POSI+IVE
THOUGHTS
POWERFUL
LIFE

Roger Fritz (1928–2011) was an American management consultant and the author of over 63 self-help and management development books, including *The Power of a Positive Attitude* and *What Managers Need to Know*.

POSI+IVE THOUGHTS POWERFUL LIFE

TRANSFORMING WITH OPTIMISTIC MINDSET

ROGER FRITZ

RUPA

Published by
Rupa Publications India Pvt. Ltd 2024
7/16, Ansari Road, Daryaganj
New Delhi 110002

Sales centres:
Bengaluru Chennai
Hyderabad Jaipur Kathmandu
Kolkata Mumbai Prayagraj

Edition copyright © Rupa Publications India Pvt. Ltd 2024

All rights reserved.
No part of this publication may be reproduced, transmitted,
or stored in a retrieval system, in any form or by any means, electronic,
mechanical, photocopying, recording or otherwise, without the prior
permission of the publisher.

P-ISBN: 978-93-5702-867-7
E-ISBN: 978-93-5702-962-9

First impression 2024

10 9 8 7 6 5 4 3 2 1

Printed in India

This book is sold subject to the condition that it shall not, by way of
trade or otherwise, be lent, resold, hired out, or otherwise circulated,
without the publisher's prior consent, in any form of binding or
cover other than that in which it is published.

CONTENTS

1	Interpreting Your World	7
2	Effective Leaders Are Positive	37
3	How Attitude Affects Results	54
4	Maximizing Your Performance	76
5	Sharpening Your Interpersonal Skills	90
6	Conquering Burnout and Stress	97
7	Upgrading Capabilities	116
8	Overcoming Problems Together	156
9	Motivating Others	172
10	Positive Attitude—the Key to Success	212

1

INTERPRETING YOUR WORLD

> *'Any fact facing us is not as important as our attitude toward it, for that determines our success or failure.'*
>
> —NORMAN VINCENT PEALE

Beginning the quest for a positive mindset requires an essential initial stage: recognizing and understanding the authentic nature of one's present attitude. However, this self-reflective endeavour frequently unfolds as more intricate than expected. Nevertheless, individuals' responses to various situations act as a reflection, mirroring their core attitude towards life.

Thriving in any pursuit or endeavour invariably hinges upon cultivating a positive or affirmative disposition as the foundational bedrock. This disposition operates as a catalytic force, moulding the perceptual lens through which challenges are perceived and addressed. It stands as a guiding beacon, directing actions and reactions towards constructive and optimistic trajectories.

Within this transformative journey, self-awareness assumes a pivotal role. It entails delving beneath the surface, unraveling the nuanced layers woven within one's responses to varying circumstances. These instinctive reactions offer glimpses into the underlying attitude—whether it inclines towards resilience, optimism, cynicism or defeatism.

Grasping the genuine nature of one's attitude necessitates a concerted effort to decipher the intricate thought patterns, emotional reactions and behavioural cues exhibited across diverse scenarios. This involves dedicated sessions of self-reflection, astute observation of personal responses and an impartial, open-minded approach towards evaluating them.

Additionally, nurturing a positive attitude involves a purposeful dedication to reframing perspectives, honing in on opportunities within adversities and adopting a proactive stance when faced with challenges. This entails fostering an optimistic outlook that actively seeks solutions instead of dwelling on problems, thereby empowering individuals to confront obstacles with unwavering resilience and steadfast determination.

Furthermore, cultivating a positive mindset demands a willingness to embrace change and adapt to the ever-evolving landscape of circumstances. It involves acknowledging the profound impact of attitude in shaping the outcomes we encounter, thereby igniting a conscious effort to harness positivity as a propelling force for personal growth and achieving success.

The journey towards fostering a positive attitude unfurls through the avenues of self-awareness, introspection and a deliberate choice to perceive life through the lens of optimism. It represents a transformative process that necessitates mindful observation, a proactive approach and an unwavering commitment to continual self-improvement. Ultimately, cultivating a positive attitude isn't merely an initial step; rather, it's an ongoing expedition—a perpetual odyssey that leads to personal empowerment, fortified resilience and a significantly more gratifying existence.

YOUR POSITIVE ATTITUDE QUOTIENT (PAQ)

Let's delve further into the process of assessing your Positive Attitude Quotient (PAQ) using a series of ten probing questions meticulously designed to gauge the frequency of positive behaviours you exhibit.

The evaluation of your PAQ centres around ten carefully crafted inquiries, each aimed at unveiling how often you display positive behaviours in your day-to-day life. This serves as a tool for self-reflection, offering insights into the consistency and patterns of your positive attitude across various situations.

Employing a scoring system—ranging from 1 for 'never' to 5 for 'almost always'—this assessment captures the range of your responses to each behaviour. Honesty and self-awareness play pivotal roles in this assessment, as the accuracy of your self-assessment significantly influences the overall determination of your PAQ.

As you navigate through the questionnaire, contemplate each question with deep thought and objectivity. Recollect instances where you've encountered similar scenarios and assess your typical response. Whether it involves spontaneous acts of kindness, maintaining an optimistic outlook during adversity or retaining composure under stress, each behaviour warrants meticulous consideration based on your regular conduct.

Following the completion of the questionnaire, the cumulative total of the scores assigned to each behaviour offers a quantitative measure of your PAQ. It's essential to acknowledge that this evaluation isn't solely about the final score; rather, it serves as a tool for self-assessment and self-awareness, aiding in comprehending your inclination towards positive behaviour.

This introspective exercise serves as the groundwork for personal enhancement and self-growth. It acts as a stepping stone, highlighting areas where consistent positive behaviour prevails and areas that offer opportunities for improvement. Embracing a candid and impartial approach to this evaluation fosters a deeper understanding of your PAQ, empowering you to embark on a journey of self-improvement and cultivating a more optimistic perspective on life.

I can quickly recover from failure. _____

I have personal goals I am working on. _____

I keep track of my progress on goals and make the changes needed. _____

I make up my mind slowly whether or not I will like new people I meet. _____

I get a lot of good ideas from other people. _____

I can find what I need to know without much help. _____

I don't have to be reminded to do what I agree to do. _____

I can quickly detect people who are pessimists. _____

I enjoy listening to people's explanations, even if I don't like them personally. _____

I am patient with people who disagree with me. _____

Total: _____

The overall score obtained from the PAQ stands as a metric, gauging the breadth and influence of your positive attitude across diverse spheres of life. It encapsulates not only your individual demeanour but also the potential impact it holds within interpersonal relationships and professional settings.

Achieving a score of 40 or higher signifies a notably robust and resilient positive attitude. This elevated level of positivity not only fortifies your credibility as a leader but also enhances your compatibility as a colleague. Such a disposition functions as a guiding light, emitting waves of optimism and resilience, fostering a climate of trust and serving as an inspiration for others to embrace a similar positive outlook.

A score falling within the range of 30 to 40 indicates a commendable yet normal level of positive attitude. It suggests room for further enhancement while reflecting a positive influence on those around you. This level of positivity lays the foundation for constructive interactions, cultivating an environment where optimism and productive thinking thrive.

However, a score ranging from 20 to 30 signifies a somewhat inconsistent attitude, potentially leading to confusion and uncertainty within relationships, both personal and professional. This range highlights the necessity for a more steadfast and deliberate approach in nurturing and maintaining a positive outlook, fostering stability and conducive conditions for growth and collaboration.

A score below 20 indicates a negative attitude, hindering confidence within relationships and hindering collaborative efforts. This range often impedes personal development and undermines collaborative endeavours. Addressing this deficit in positivity becomes essential to cultivate healthier relationships and a more fruitful work environment.

Employing the PAQ scale as a guiding compass facilitates introspection, shedding light on areas that necessitate focussed efforts toward enhancing positivity. It assists in identifying specific facets of attitude that require attention and refinement.

By pinpointing these areas, individuals can embark on a purposeful journey of self-improvement, nurturing a more positive attitude that not only fosters personal growth but also positively influences their surroundings.

ASSESS YOUR ATTITUDE TOWARD YOURSELF

The undeniable significance of physical well-being on life quality is a recognized truth. However, the pivotal factor often influencing overall life quality is the attitude one adopts. This attitude isn't confined to internal realms but extends outward, shaping interactions with others and molding the surrounding environment.

For cultivating a positive attitude towards oneself, introspection plays a pivotal role. A series of introspective questions serves as a roadmap, offering insights into the orientation of one's attitude:

1. **Learner or Rejecter:** recognizing life's inherent complexity and fostering an attitude of continuous learning and adaptation is crucial. Are you open to acknowledging that nobody holds all the answers, fostering a mindset of ongoing learning and perseverance?
2. **Effort at Work:** beyond task completion, a positive attitude is evident in the proactive endeavour to propose improvements and enrich the work atmosphere. Are you consistently striving to excel, displaying enthusiasm for discovering more efficient ways to accomplish tasks?
3. **Demonstration of Enthusiasm:** enthusiasm becomes a beacon, radiating positivity in both words and actions. Reflect on the impressions you leave on others—do your

actions and conversations convey enthusiasm? Seeking feedback from friends can provide a comprehensive perspective.
4. **Willingness to Grow:** embracing a positive attitude entails taking charge of personal growth and advancement. Are you proactive in preparing yourself for progress, or do you rely solely on external guidance for direction?
5. **Embracing Change:** positivity manifests in an open-mindedness toward change, a willingness to experiment and an eagerness to entertain new ideas. Are you open and proactive in embracing change and exploring new approaches?
6. **Cultivating Humor and Joy:** finally, fostering a positive attitude involves nurturing a sense of humour, refraining from taking oneself too seriously, and deriving joy from work. Do you infuse a sense of lightness and enjoyment into your endeavours?

These questions serve as a mirror, reflecting one's self-attitude and aiding in identifying areas where a shift in perspective or approach might prove beneficial. Embracing a positive attitude isn't merely about self-transformation but also about shaping interactions and cultivating a more conducive environment that nurtures growth, collaboration, and fulfillment.

EVALUATE YOUR ATTITUDE TOWARD OTHER PEOPLE

'Attitude is a little thing that makes a big difference.'

—WINSTON CHURCHILL

Assessing one's consistent positive attitude towards others necessitates a comprehensive and multifaceted approach. Below are several facets to consider when evaluating this perspective:

1. **Genuine Interest:** an authentic positive attitude towards others originates from a sincere interest and genuine concern for their well-being. Are you actively engaged in conversations, genuinely discussing their needs and concerns without pretense? Authenticity in interactions cannot be fabricated but resonates through true empathy and care.
2. **Empathetic Understanding:** nurturing a positive attitude towards others entails embracing empathy. Do you make an effort to comprehend their viewpoints, emotions and motivations? This involves delving deeper into their feelings, understanding why they feel a certain way and deciphering the reasoning behind their actions. Being an attentive and empathetic listener plays a pivotal role in fostering positive relationships.
3. **Collaborative Mindset:** collaboration forms the cornerstone of a positive attitude towards others. Are you skilled in working cooperatively with individuals to accomplish shared objectives? A positive attitude is manifested in being a team player, prioritizing collective goals over personal agendas and cultivating an environment of mutual respect and support.

Moreover, nurturing a consistently positive attitude towards others extends beyond these considerations, encompassing actions and behaviours pivotal in fostering a harmonious and supportive environment:

1. **Demonstrating Support:** are you proactive in extending

assistance and support to those in your circle? A positive attitude often manifests in actions that uplift others, providing help when needed and readily extending a helping hand without hesitation.
2. **Encouragement and Acknowledgment:** positivity flourishes through encouragement and acknowledgment. Do you actively recognize and commend the efforts and achievements of others? Cultivating a habit of acknowledging and celebrating accomplishments nurtures a culture of positivity and motivates continued growth.
3. **Conflict Resolution:** approaching conflicts with a positive attitude holds paramount importance. Are you adept at managing disagreements or conflicts with a constructive and solution-oriented approach? A positive attitude involves seeking resolutions that benefit all involved parties, promoting understanding and fostering compromise.

By introspecting on these facets, individuals can gauge the depth and consistency of their positive attitude towards others. The goal extends beyond self-reflection, aiming to cultivate an environment where positivity permeates interactions, nurturing mutual respect, empathy and collaboration for collective growth and harmonious coexistence.

ATTITUDE REFLECTS POSITIVELY AND NEGATIVELY

The profound impact of attitude on personal and professional realms is undeniable. Delving deeper into the realm of workplace safety, it becomes evident that attitude plays a pivotal role in shaping behaviours that can either fortify or undermine the safety fabric within an organizational setting.

When it comes to workplace safety, a negative attitude holds the potential to engender a spectrum of detrimental behaviours. These behaviours not only endanger individual well-being but also pose a threat to the collective safety of the work environment. This negative mindset often breeds a sense of complacency and disregard, ultimately leading to actions that compromise safety protocols.

1. Carelessness emerges as a prominent trait associated with a negative attitude toward workplace safety. This manifests as a casual indifference to safety protocols, with individuals expressing sentiments such as, 'It's not a big deal' or 'It won't make a difference', indicating a lack of concern for potential hazards and safety measures.
2. Ignorance becomes a byproduct of dismissive attitudes, leading individuals to overlook crucial safety information. Statements like, 'I didn't realize that could be dangerous' or 'I wasn't aware of the risks involved' showcase a lack of attentiveness or interest in adhering to established safety guidelines.
3. Fatalism ingrains itself within a negative attitude, resulting in an acceptance of potential risks without proactive risk prevention measures. Attitudes reflecting sentiments like, 'If something bad happens, it's meant to b' or 'There's no escaping fate' demonstrate a resigned acceptance of hazards rather than a proactive approach to prevent them.
4. Cynicism surfaces as scepticism toward safety measures, undermining their significance. Such attitudes tend to belittle safety training efforts, dismissing them as trivial or unnecessary. Phrases like 'All this safety talk is pointless' or

'It's just a waste of time' downplay the importance of safety protocols.
5. Laziness permeates through a negative attitude, leading individuals to neglect safety gear or precautions. This stems from considering safety measures as inconvenient hurdles rather than crucial safeguards. Attitudes expressed as 'I don't feel like bothering with this safety gear' or 'It's too much hassle' highlight a disregard for necessary precautions.
6. Recklessness and Overconfidence surface as a result of dismissive attitudes, promoting risky behaviours. Statements such as, 'Taking risks makes life interesting' or 'I thrive on living dangerously' showcase a false sense of invincibility or a penchant for seeking thrill, disregarding the potential dangers involved.

A positive approach towards workplace safety serves as the bedrock for cultivating a culture steeped in vigilance, responsibility and proactive commitment. This mindset stands in stark contrast to its negative counterpart, emphasizing the crucial role of positivity in fostering an environment conducive to safety and well-being.

1. Planning and Diligence stand as hallmarks of a positive attitude towards workplace safety. This mindset champions meticulous planning and adherence to safety protocols, placing paramount importance on executing tasks following the right procedures to safeguard the welfare of all involved.
2. Encouragement and Support emerge as pillars of a positive safety culture, advocating for a collaborative approach among team members. This entails encouraging open dialogue to articulate safety objectives and providing unwavering support for one another's safety endeavours,

fostering a spirit of collective improvement.
3. Appreciation and Gratitude form the cornerstone of a positive safety environment. Acknowledging contributions and suggestions becomes customary, nurturing a culture where expressions like, 'Thank you for that insightful suggestion' reverberate, reinforcing the value of active participation in safety measures.
4. Thoroughness and Care become ingrained in the positive outlook, highlighting the significance of meticulous task execution. This approach emphasizes completing tasks with utmost care and precision to avert potential safety hazards, ensuring that tasks are done accurately the first time to mitigate any risk of harm.
5. Conscientiousness and Responsibility epitomize the essence of a positive attitude towards safety. It involves a proactive stance, swiftly taking action to rectify potential hazards, showcasing a conscientious attitude aimed at preventing accidents before they materialize.
6. Alertness and Focus serve as byproducts of a positive mindset, fostering a culture of mindfulness and attentiveness. This heightened awareness underscores a continuous focus on safety measures, benefitting the collective well-being of all involved parties.
7. Ultimately, embracing a positive attitude towards workplace safety transcends individual well-being. It serves as a catalyst for nurturing a collaborative and safety-oriented environment, where the collective safety and welfare of all stakeholders stand at the forefront of daily operations.

Success doesn't hinge solely upon talent and knowledge; rather, it's deeply intertwined with one's state of mind and attitude: the path to success is a complex one, encompassing not just inherent talent or accumulated knowledge but also the indispensable aspects of mindset and attitude. While talent and knowledge lay the groundwork, it's the state of mind that serves as the driving force, determining how one's potential is realized. A positive mindset plays a pivotal role as a force multiplier, elevating reliability, nurturing respect and fostering an environment that nurtures success.

A positive mental outlook inherently fosters a sense of dependability. Positivity infuses individuals with a consistent and trustworthy approach, augmenting their commitment and accountability. This reliability extends beyond task completion; it manifests in the respect and consideration one extends to others. A positive mindset inherently compels individuals to honour and appreciate others' contributions, cultivating a culture of mutual esteem and support.

Additionally, taking pride in one's work and recognizing others' achievements are intrinsic features of a positive mindset. This mindset cultivates a sense of ownership and accountability toward one's tasks, while also acknowledging the efforts and accomplishments of colleagues. Collaborative enthusiasm and the inclination to offer assistance emerge naturally from a positive mindset, as individuals actively seek avenues to enhance collective efficiency and share their enthusiasm with peers.

Simple yet impactful gestures, such as a smile, become potent tools for imparting encouragement to others. A positive demeanour exudes contagious energy, uplifting the spirits of those nearby and sparking a chain reaction of motivation and optimism. This shared encouragement often loops back, reinforcing the positive cycle and fostering a nurturing work environment.

Recognizing the pivotal role of one's internal landscape in shaping attitudes holds immense importance. The initial step in evaluating and improving attitude typically commences with introspection. Acknowledging that the most formidable obstacles often stem from within prompts a proactive approach toward self-reflection and personal growth. This self-awareness serves as the cornerstone in nurturing a positive mindset—one that not only propels individual success but also significantly contributes to fostering a harmonious and productive collective environment.

In essence, success goes beyond mere talent and knowledge; it's the convergence of skills, mindset and attitude. A positive state of mind acts as a catalyst, amplifying the impact of talent and knowledge, while fostering respect, collaboration and motivation within oneself and among peers, laying the groundwork for mutual growth and accomplishment.

MAKE UP YOUR MIND TO BE POSITIVE

*'All human beings can alter their lives
by altering their attitudes.'*

—ANDREW CARNEGIE

Finding delight in life's simple pleasures holds the potential for a profound shift toward embracing contentment. It involves embracing gratitude for the present while recognizing life's amalgamation of highs and lows. No individual possesses an abundance of everything; however, each person carries unique moments of joy and sorrow. The key lies in tipping the scales in favour of laughter, allowing it to outweigh tears by relishing the small moments of joy that life unfolds.

Adapting to circumstances and acknowledging the unpredictability of the future stands as a crucial element in leading a fulfilling life. Attempting to avoid all risks or seeking complete immunity from misfortunes proves impractical. Recognizing life's uncertainties empowers individuals to confront challenges with resilience and flexibility.

The weight of external opinions and societal norms often burdens decision-making processes. Learning to filter excessive criticism and refusing to let external influences dictate life choices brings liberation. Authenticity in actions and decisions fosters lasting fulfillment. Embracing individuality and pursuing activities that bring personal satisfaction nurtures a sense of contentment and purpose.

Envy and grudges erode the soul, impeding personal growth. Embracing a mindset free from jealousy and resentment creates room for positivity and development. Steering clear of toxic relationships and cultivating diverse interests expands horizons, even when immediate travel isn't feasible. Engaging in hobbies, delving into literature or learning about new places fosters a sense of adventure and enrichment.

Reflecting excessively on past mistakes or regretting missed opportunities can impede personal progress. Redirecting energy toward learning from past experiences, without dwelling excessively on regrets, becomes a pathway for individual growth and resilience. Avoiding unnecessary self-blame or overthinking prevents being consumed by sorrow or excessive self-criticism.

Essentially, discovering contentment amidst life's intricacies involves cherishing simplicity, resilience in the face of adversity and the bravery to carve one's own journey. It's about embracing gratitude, living authentically, nurturing positive emotions and steering clear of negative influences to lead a richly fulfilling life brimming with happiness and purpose.

Frequently, individuals find themselves entangled in the past, holding onto grudges or lingering in moments of regret. Observing those around us who dwell on past grievances can serve as a reflection, prompting contemplation on the impacts of such attitudes. Evaluating whether such attitudes breed positivity or negativity can guide our own inclinations toward healthier mindsets.

A potent method to counteract negativity and cultivate contentment is extending a helping hand to those less fortunate. Engaging in acts of kindness not only benefits others but also fosters a sense of gratitude and purpose within oneself. Moreover, staying actively involved in multiple pursuits acts as a shield against unhappiness. Keeping busy often catalyzes productivity and joy, leaving minimal space for negativity to seep in.

In moments of self-doubt or uncertainty, it's vital to recognize that life is an ongoing journey, not a fixed destination. Embracing this outlook encourages acceptance of life's continual ebb and flow. The pursuit of conclusions is perpetual, characterized by constant adjustments in response to changes, fears, failures or even successes.

Novel experiences often bring a blend of excitement and risk. Adapting to unfamiliar situations or diverse individuals necessitates flexibility and emotional equilibrium. Maintaining emotional composure, especially in professional settings, stands as a crucial skill for acclimatizing to new environments. Furthermore, evaluating personal routines and actively seeking methods to break potential monotony contributes to personal growth and adaptability.

The concept of self-perception holds significant sway over life's outcomes. How individuals view themselves directly impacts their attitudes, behaviours, and eventual achievements. Nurturing a positive self-image can act as a catalyst for cultivating a constructive attitude, leading to actions that pave the way for success and personal fulfillment.

Embracing resilience, fostering adaptability and nurturing a positive self-view are crucial in navigating life's complexities. Observing the repercussions of negative attitudes, extending kindness to others, staying engaged in activities, embracing life as an ongoing journey and fostering a positive self-image are fundamental elements that contribute to a purposeful and satisfying life journey.

The essence of confidence, garnering respect and effecting positive change largely hinges on nurturing and maintaining a healthy self-view. Unfortunately, many of us fall short in this regard due to a lack of consistent daily self-image upkeep. This deficiency often arises from a reactive approach to life rather than an assertive and proactive stance.

An analogy that illustrates the importance of self-image maintenance is likening it to tending a crop. Just as a farmer can't control the weather but can impact the quality of their crop through diligent care, individuals can shape their self-worth, confidence and opportunities by focusing on controllable aspects. This shift highlights the significance of taking charge of actionable steps rather than fixating on uncontrollable external factors.

The inclination to attribute blame to external circumstances, indulge in self-pity, seek revenge or dwell on past mistakes saps valuable time and energy. The key lies in acknowledging doubts and fears without letting them hinder progress. However, genuine change doesn't arise solely from introspection or analysis—it requires active measures. Deliberate actions taken toward improvement spark real transformation.

Implementing change isn't a straightforward or effortless endeavour; it demands unwavering determination and disciplined efforts. It necessitates a steadfast commitment to step outside the comfort zone and embrace discomfort, recognizing that growth and progress often stem from moments of challenge and adversity.

In short, cultivating a robust self-image entails a conscious and intentional effort toward proactive action rather than reactive responses. It involves a shift in mindset—from attributing blame to external factors to focusing on personal agency and control. By channeling energy into actionable steps, acknowledging and addressing doubts and fears and embracing disciplined efforts for self-improvement, individuals can pave the way for lasting confidence, self-worth and positive transformations.

CHANGE THE WAY YOU FEEL ABOUT YOURSELF

'The only disability in life is a bad attitude.'

—SCOTT HAMILTON

Revamping one's self-perception is a transformative journey that holds the potential to profoundly impact personal growth and well-being. Here are several empowering strategies to kickstart positive changes in self-perception:

1. **Unburden from the Past:** embracing personal liberation involves acknowledging past mistakes and releasing their hold. Symbolizing this release, such as writing down past

liabilities and letting them go, actively signifies your intent to shed the weight of past shortcomings. Learning from these experiences is crucial, but freeing yourself from their burden is equally essential. Recognizing that dwelling on past mistakes impedes progress reinforces the necessity of moving forward.

2. **Acknowledge Your Value:** recognizing your strengths, competencies and achievements is paramount. Creating a realistic and affirming résumé or catalogue of personal attributes highlights your inherent value. Consistently reinforcing these positive attributes through repetition and acknowledgment solidifies a robust self-image. Redirecting thoughts to positive aspects encourages a shift toward a more confident and empowered self-perception.

3. **Engage with Positivity:** actively seeking motivational or inspirational content enriches the mind and spirit. Exposure to positive examples, experiences and wisdom from others serves as a catalyst for personal development. Learning from others' successes and strategies accelerates progress, offering invaluable insights and minimizing the trial-and-error process.

4. **Establish Concrete Goals:** setting specific, written goals triggers your subconscious goal-seeking mechanism. This subconscious reinforcement aids in surmounting obstacles, as your mind diligently strives to achieve these defined objectives. Every accomplished goal provides tangible evidence of your progress, reinforcing belief in your capabilities and nurturing a positive self-image.

5. **Curate Your Emotional Environment:** taking charge of your emotional landscape involves consciously selecting positive influences. Surrounding yourself with supportive,

uplifting individuals creates a nurturing environment conducive to personal growth. Understanding that your emotional surroundings significantly shape your mindset underscores the importance of choosing associations that align with your aspirations.

Every stride in this transformative journey signifies a deliberate endeavour towards self-liberation and empowerment. Releasing the burdens of the past, recognizing your inherent worth, seeking positive influences, delineating precise objectives and cultivating a supportive environment propel you on a path that not only reshapes your self-view but also propels you toward personal contentment and success.

Although these initial strides might seem uncomplicated, their simplicity doesn't diminish their profound impact. They serve as the cornerstone upon which a sturdy and resilient self-perception can be constructed. Supported by empirical research, these foundational steps have exhibited significant outcomes in various studies and personal narratives.

At their essence, these actions establish the framework for nurturing what I term as internal net worth—an amalgamation of your beliefs, values and self-perception. This internal wealth cannot be measured in material terms but holds immeasurable significance in shaping your mindset, behaviours and interactions with the world.

Believing in and nurturing your strengths and core principles isn't merely a superficial exercise; it's a profound commitment to self-awareness and self-acceptance. It's about recognizing your capabilities, talents and virtues, embracing them as the bedrock of your identity.

Moreover, assuming accountability for your worth and

competence as an active and accomplished individual is pivotal. Embracing this responsibility signifies a shift from a passive standpoint to an empowered mindset. It involves acknowledging that your choices, actions and beliefs lie within your control, setting the stage for personal responsibility and advancement.

This journey of transformation, aimed at nurturing a positive self-image, doesn't occur in isolation; its effects reverberate outward, impacting those in your sphere. As you cement your belief in yourself, uphold your values and take ownership of your path, you inherently emit this positivity. Your conduct and demeanour serve as a source of inspiration, influencing others through your actions.

Truly, these initial strides lay the foundation for a profound personal metamorphosis. As you internalize these beliefs and values, they not only shape your personal trajectory but also position you as a beacon of positivity and empowerment for those around you. These steps transcend mere self-betterment; they act as the catalyst for a ripple effect, fostering positive change within yourself and emanating outward, affecting the world around you.

PULL YOURSELF UP

'Those who keep trying can renew themselves.'

The pursuit of long-lasting success unfolds as a journey characterized by gradual advancements rather than sudden, overnight triumphs. It's comparable to embarking on a climb up a ladder where each step, each rung, symbolizes a distinct phase of growth and learning. The narrative of baseball icon Eddie Matthews stands as an inspiring testament to this steady path towards success.

Eddie Matthews, a towering figure in baseball history, didn't soar to greatness overnight. His story vividly illustrates the invaluable lesson of commencing from humble beginnings, often at the ladder's base, and methodically ascending, step by step. Matthews didn't vault into fame and acclaim; instead, he meticulously honed his skills, encountered challenges and persistently toiled his way upward on the ladder of success.

His journey epitomizes the dedication, resilience and perseverance demanded to navigate the complexities of a chosen field or pursuit. Matthews didn't sidestep the indispensable phases of growth and development; rather, he embraced each stage, amassing experiences and refining his expertise along the journey.

By spotlighting Matthews' trajectory, we acknowledge the significance of patience and tenacity in achieving enduring success. His narrative underscores the essence of embracing the process, respecting the journey and recognizing that true accomplishment often necessitates consistent effort and gradual advancement.

Matthews' tale serves as a poignant reminder that genuine, enduring success isn't an immediate destination; instead, it emerges from persistent effort, learning from setbacks and steadily ascending the ladder of progress, rung by rung.

Eddie Matthews' pivotal decision at the crossroads of his baseball career reveals a profound wisdom that transcends the allure of an instant hefty signing bonus. Despite the stark contrast between the lucrative offer from the Brooklyn Dodgers and the comparatively modest one from the Boston Braves, Matthews' discerning judgment guided him along the less-traveled path.

Initially, opting for the Braves' offer might have appeared

as a financial compromise, yet Matthews possessed a deeper comprehension of his abilities and the genuine essence of achieving success. His precocious foresight and maturity at a young age enabled him to perceive the long-term significance of his decision, transcending the immediate financial gain.

By selecting the Braves and their minor league teams, Matthews consciously prioritized the pursuit of knowledge and personal development over immediate gratification. He grasped that true mastery in baseball—or any pursuit for that matter—required more than mere monetary rewards; it necessitated commitment, hands-on experience and a profound immersion in the game's intricacies.

The period spent in the minor leagues played a pivotal role in Matthews' journey. It acted as an invaluable training arena where he not only refined his athletic abilities but also imbibed invaluable life lessons from seasoned veterans whose careers were approaching closure. Being in proximity to these former major league stars served as an apprenticeship, providing insights beyond the technicalities of the game.

Immersing himself in this environment allowed Matthews to absorb essential principles of success: the ethos of giving his utmost effort every day, upholding humility and fostering an unwavering dedication to triumph. This foundational experience laid the groundwork for his future accomplishments in baseball and his endeavours beyond the baseball diamond.

Matthews' choice to forgo immediate gains in favour of long-term development epitomizes the sagacity of investing in one's personal growth and education. It transcended the act of simply playing the game; it encompassed understanding the core of success, refining character and cultivating a mindset that surpassed the confines of the game. This formative phase in the minor leagues ultimately emerged as the cornerstone of his illustrious career.

Eddie Matthews' career achievements serve as a testament to the wisdom and foresight underlying his decision to commence in the minor leagues. His remarkable tally of 512 home runs, positioning him in a tie with the esteemed Ernie Banks for thirteenth on the all-time career home run list, underscores his mastery on the baseball field.

Matthews' career shone brightly with an array of milestones that vividly showcased the depth of his exceptional talent and unwavering dedication. His remarkable achievement of hitting thirty or more home runs in nine consecutive seasons stands as an unparalleled record—a testament to his unwavering consistency and excellence on the field. Furthermore, his impressive knack for achieving forty or more home runs on four separate occasions solidifies his legacy as an eminent and prolific home run hitter. Additionally, his participation in ten All-Star games unequivocally underscores his esteemed status among the pantheon of baseball's elite players.

Of notable significance, Matthews' induction into the National Baseball Hall of Fame in 1978 firmly cemented his position among the most revered legends of the sport, honouring his enduring impact and stellar contributions to the game's history and evolution.

Furthermore, recent research conducted by the University of Minnesota provides empirical validation to the trajectory of Matthews' early career. This study emphasizes the advantages that young individuals derive from engaging in part-time employment during their formative years. It underscores the invaluable lessons acquired through such experiences, encompassing adeptness in time management, budgeting, financial literacy, interpersonal skills and effectively navigating work-related stress. This revelation serves as a testament to the enduring benefits reaped from acquiring skills and experiences at an early age.

Matthews' deliberate choice to commence his career in the minor leagues not only laid the solid groundwork for his illustrious journey in baseball but also harmonizes with contemporary research affirming the advantages of early exposure to work experiences. His narrative resonates as a compelling testament to the sustained advantages of learning and acquiring crucial skills during youth, offering individuals a robust foundation and enduring resilience as they traverse their professional paths.

REWORK MISTAKES

Richard Wagner's rise to global recognition as a composer challenges the conventional belief that success stems solely from inherent talent. Despite his passion for theater, art and music, Wagner's journey deviated from the expected trajectory. Contrary to the archetype of a prodigy, he grappled with constraints: an aversion to being onstage, modest drawing skills limited to stick figures and a slow grasp of piano playing. Yet, his sheer determination overshadowed any perceived absence of natural talent.

At a tender age of fifteen, Wagner dared to dream of a career as a composer. Instead of relying solely on his innate abilities, he embarked on an unconventional path of relentless self-education. He plunged into the depths of libraries, immersing himself in a composition book, committing its contents to memory and using it as a launchpad toward his aspirations.

To refine his musical expertise, he sought guidance beyond traditional schooling. He engaged a violinist from the Leipzig Orchestra to enlighten him on chords and keys intricacies. Wagner's thirst for knowledge led him to meticulously study the technical aspects of every orchestral instrument, comprehending their subtleties and capabilities, except for the harp. His deep dive into the works of revered composers like Beethoven was not passive admiration but a quest to unlock their mastery and decipher the secrets behind capturing distinct sounds.

Wagner's systematic approach stands as evidence of his unwavering determination. He didn't solely rely on his inherent talents but actively pursued mentors, absorbed information voraciously and dissected the compositions of musical maestros to unravel the intricacies of composing.

His story serves as a compelling narrative, showcasing that while innate talent might offer an advantage, persistence, resilience and an insatiable thirst for knowledge can triumph over perceived limitations. Wagner's journey illustrates the potency of dedication and self-education in overcoming obstacles and carving an enduring legacy in the realm of music.

Richard Wagner's initial attempts at composing music were met with mockery rather than applause. When he first presented his musical creations to an audience, the unexpected reaction was not praise but laughter, a humbling experience for the seventeen-year-old composer who, overwhelmed by embarrassment, discreetly exited the theater.

Confronted with this setback, Wagner demonstrated an extraordinary level of humility and a readiness to learn from critique. Seeking guidance from a local church musician, he received invaluable advice: before delving into uncharted territories, he needed a firm grasp of the fundamentals of music composition. Embracing this counsel, he meticulously analysed the compositions of iconic figures like Bach and Mozart, dissecting their musical pieces line by line. Through this painstaking process, he gradually refined his ability to craft melodious and coherent musical phrases.

Armed with newfound knowledge and a determination to perfect his art, Wagner seized a second opportunity to showcase his work to an audience. This time, his compositions resonated with listeners, marking a turning point in his career trajectory. This pivotal moment not only validated his potential but also set the stage for his ascent in the music realm.

Furthermore, Wagner's openness to drawing inspiration from unconventional sources serves as a testament to his innovative spirit. A striking incident underscores his exceptional adaptability and creativity: amid the discordant sounds of a neighbor hammering tin downstairs while he composed, instead of being deterred, Wagner ingeniously integrated the cacophony into his music. This unique fusion eventually found its place as a significant segment in his renowned opera, *Siegfried*.

Wagner's readiness to embrace criticism, combined with his relentless pursuit of improvement and a remarkable ability to derive inspiration from the most unexpected sources, showcases the resilience and ingenuity that defined his artistic journey. His experiences underscore the invaluable lessons in humility, adaptability and perseverance that significantly contributed to his eventual success in the world of music.

Philip Knight, the visionary behind Nike, fervently believed that driving transformative efforts for his business offered more personal fulfillment than the routine operations of a vast corporation. As a result, he handed over this responsibility to another leader. Following suit, luminaries like Bill Gates and Donald Dell followed similar paths. While Steve Jobs faced a setback at Apple Computer due to a delayed response, leading to potential ousting by shareholders, he resolutely made a triumphant comeback, driven by an unwavering determination to elevate the company to unprecedented heights—a mission in which he unequivocally succeeded.

Likewise, the journeys of Bill Gates and Donald Dell underscore the concept that a change in roles often aligns with a broader vision. Their acknowledgment that steering a company's long-term trajectory might require a fresh perspective underscores the importance of adaptability in leadership. By stepping away from day-to-day tasks, they fostered a flow of new ideas and strategies that propelled their ventures to new levels.

Steve Jobs' story embodies resilience and the unyielding drive to reclaim a legacy. His departure from and subsequent return to Apple illustrate the intricacies of corporate dynamics. Jobs' comeback, fueled by unwavering determination, epitomizes the fusion of innovation, leadership and sheer determination. His pivotal role in reshaping Apple's trajectory underscores the impact of a visionary leader who transcended setbacks to achieve unparalleled success.

Collectively, these stories shed light on the intricate balance between visionary leadership, strategic delegation and the pursuit of innovation. They serve as profound examples of how navigating the interplay between delegating day-to-day operations and charting a visionary path can redefine the course of iconic companies and shape entire industries.

LOOK FOR A BETTER WAY

The unyielding determination of Chester Carlson stands as a resounding testament to the transformative power of resilience amidst adversity. His life's journey embodies how the right attitude, fortified by unwavering perseverance, can transform setbacks into stepping stones towards unparalleled success.

Carlson's life was shaped by early responsibilities thrust upon him due to familial circumstances, forging a steadfast resolve within him. The challenges he faced, such as caring for his invalid parents at a young age and enduring their untimely passing, instilled in him a tenacity that propelled his progress. These adversities served as the crucible where his unwavering determination was honed.

His pursuit of education amid these trials, culminating in a physics degree from Cal Tech, reflected his resolute perseverance. Despite facing rejection from numerous firms—totalling eighty-two—these setbacks only fuelled his determination. His brief employment at Bell Labs, followed by a layoff in 1933, marked the beginning of his transformative journey.

Rather than succumb to despair, Carlson embarked on a solitary endeavour, conducting experiments within the confines of his modest apartment's kitchen. Despite enduring excruciating pain caused by arthritis, he channelled his suffering into an unwavering quest for a solution. His daily struggle of manually copying drawings intensified the agony, spurring his determination to innovate a better alternative.

In 1938, Carlson, alongside Otto Kornei, introduced the first office copier, marking a revolutionary breakthrough. Yet, the path to recognition was riddled with rejection. Initially, twenty companies, including industry giants like General Electric, RCA and IBM, rejected Carlson's innovation. However, the eventual acquisition of his invention by Haloid in 1946, later rebranded as Xerox in 1958, stands as a testament to the monumental success derived from Carlson's unwavering perseverance.

Chester Carlson's story vividly illustrates how facing adversity with resilience and an unyielding spirit can become the forge for ground-breaking innovation and monumental achievements. His life's journey stands as an enduring testament to the transformative potential of determination and the relentless pursuit of one's vision, especially when confronted with seemingly insurmountable challenges.

'Hoping and wishing are never enough. Change and improvement come only when determination sparks action.'

2

EFFECTIVE LEADERS ARE POSITIVE

'Looking back with regrets is a dangerous and self-defeating habit because it prevents a positive attitude. Move on!'

The insights derived from both triumphs and setbacks intertwine closely with one's mindset. Whether you occupy the pinnacle as a CEO, diligently contribute as a mail clerk or exist somewhere in between these roles, emulating the qualities demonstrated by triumphant leaders holds immeasurable value.

Upon delving into the characteristics that define successful leaders, it becomes evident how pivotal a positive attitude is in their accomplishments. These pioneering figures encompass an array of traits:

- They demonstrate an admirable ability to withstand frustration, navigating challenges with unwavering resilience.
- They encourage active involvement from others stands as a cornerstone of their leadership approach.
- Their continuous self-reflection propels their ongoing growth and evolution.
- Their competitiveness is defined by a blend of integrity

and grace.
- Despite impulses, they refrain from retaliatory actions, showcasing commendable self-control.
- They celebrate triumphs with humility, free from any traces of boastfulness.
- Similarly, during moments of defeat, they exhibit resilience, shunning despondency.
- Their decisions and actions are guided by an ethical, moral and legal compass.
- They are conscious of group dynamics, nurturing and valuing group loyalties.
- Realistic goal-setting forms the bedrock of their strategic approaches.

Whether at the helm of a substantial team or navigating the early stages of a career, gleaning insights from these triumphant leaders unravels the roadmap to reaching the heights of accomplishment. An integral component involves engaging in an honest self-evaluation, posing the pivotal query, 'Do I await guidance passively or seize the reins of my personal development?'

It's noteworthy that those who ascend to remarkable achievements aren't divinely ordained. Physically, emotionally and intellectually, they share similarities with the majority of us. Their personalities, levels of intelligence and approaches to pursuing objectives exhibit remarkable diversity.

Moreover, a positive attitude acts as a catalyst, not only sparking personal drive but also inspiring the same fervor in those within your sphere. Cultivating this enthusiasm for growth and achievement is facilitated when you:

- Transform ideas, whether self-conceived or from others,

into actionable plans.
- Embrace accountability for actions and decisions taken.
- Exercise sound judgment, minimizing inner conflicts.
- Prioritize facts over subjective opinions, diligently gathering and interpreting data to address problems or seize opportunities.
- Master the art of communication, creating an environment where everyone feels valued and heard.
- Recognize and appreciate the significance of others' roles and contributions to the collective effort.

Additionally, effective leaders demonstrate proficiency in interpersonal connections. Frequently, technical deficiencies aren't the primary hurdles; instead, it's the incapacity to collaborate effectively with colleagues. Those skilled at building relationships have honed the skill of earning genuine respect by:

- Treating others with the same respect they seek.
- Excelling as mentors and coaches.
- Providing constructive feedback.
- Prioritizing collective goals and harmony over personal desires.

The previously mentioned qualities offer just a glimpse into the varied array of attributes that successful leaders meticulously develop. Regardless of your current position within the organizational hierarchy, mastering these traits is not only achievable but essential for personal and professional advancement.

Exploring beyond the mentioned traits, additional crucial characteristics encapsulate the core of successful leadership. Adopting these practices requires a deliberate focus on key aspects:

articulating and clarifying new ideas or initiatives goes beyond merely presenting concepts. It involves anticipating potential obstacles, objections and concerns while empathizing with others' viewpoints on change. Recognizing and dismantling obstacles to cooperation becomes pivotal for implementing ideas effectively.

A vital part of this process involves acknowledging the limitations of absolute solutions. Shifting away from unproductive blame assignment toward constructive inquiry—solving, refining and improving—is essential.

Furthermore, fostering curiosity becomes a fundamental aspect of effective leadership. Successful leaders remain highly aware of evolving trends and advancements within their industry. Preferring insightful reading over passive TV consumption channels their energy toward high-impact priorities—an approach ripe for adoption.

Boldly embracing calculated risks involves venturing into uncharted territories, trusting individuals, navigating unconventional situations and seeking innovative solutions, even at the potential cost of job security—an audacious step toward progress.

Moreover, utilizing humor to encourage active engagement—a spirited rallying cry of 'let's do it'—becomes a powerful tool for driving change and mobilizing collective effort. These attributes are invaluable during times of transition.

Prioritizing excellence over mediocrity emerges as a crucial practice. It not only nurtures increased job satisfaction but also fuels motivation and boosts staff morale. Empowering employees to carve their career paths yields significant benefits, even for those without managerial roles. Simple gestures, like sending emails that highlight outstanding contributions, can notably elevate the workplace environment.

Embracing the wisdom encapsulated in the adage, 'A positive attitude helps us break through stalemates and progress,' embodying these qualities establishes a robust framework to navigate challenges, drive progress and propel personal and collective growth to new heights. This holistic approach forms the foundation for a transformative journey toward effective leadership and ongoing advancement.

> *'A positive attitude enables us to make up our minds against stalemates and in favour of progress.'*

BELIEVE IN YOURSELF

The foundation of maintaining a positive attitude lies in unwavering self-confidence. In these times of unpredictability and turmoil, the idea of absolute certainty appears like a mirage, slipping away from our grasp. Those who adamantly claim certainty often carry a shade of pessimism, painting a perpetually darkening picture of the future. Strangely, this negativity tends to manifest as a self-fulfilling prophecy; pessimism spreads rapidly, influencing perceptions and ultimately shaping outcomes. It's an intriguing paradox that what one deems impossible often becomes a reality, with the belief itself acting as the catalyst for its own fulfillment.

Consider the timeless tale of 'The Man Who Sold Hot Dogs', a story likely born in the 1930s but resonating through generations. Imagine a humble vendor stationed by the roadside, selling hot dogs. Deafened by hearing impairments and blind to worldly news due to vision troubles, he diligently sold his quality hot dogs. His persistent call, 'Buy a hot dog, Mister!' struck a chord, drawing in customers. Witnessing success, he expanded operations, procured more supplies and even sought help from his college-educated son. However, a turning point came when his son, armed with worldly knowledge, painted a bleak picture of global and domestic affairs. Yielding to his son's perspective, the father scaled back operations, removed signs and halted roadside sales. As expected, hot dog sales plummeted overnight. Succumbing to prevailing pessimism, the father agreed with his son's assessment, lamenting, 'You're right, son. We are indeed in the midst of a Great Depression.'

Amidst an atmosphere heavy with despair, many find themselves paralysed by uncertainty, hesitant to venture into the unknown without assurances against potential pitfalls. This is where the concept of destiny gains significance: fleeting moments of success seem insignificant compared to the enduring grasp of obscurity.

While uncertainty acts as a barrier for some, there are those who see it as an essential part of life's journey. Certainty, often perceived as a coveted treasure, lacks a solid footing in reality, much like the unpredictability of a racetrack. Life's certainties dissolve into mere probabilities. Confident individuals anticipate these probabilities, hoping that they will gradually align in their favour, similar to the ever-shifting odds in a game of chance.

This reserve of confidence doesn't rely on external validations or guarantees of safety. Instead, it springs from an unshakeable self-reliance grounded in personal convictions. It involves charting one's own course, navigating through the intricate maze of uncertainty with unwavering self-assurance. In this realm of certainty, dependency fades, replaced by an unwavering trust in one's abilities and beliefs.

> *'A happy person is not a person in a certain set of circumstances, but rather a person with a certain set of attitudes.'*
>
> —HUGH DOWNS

THE IMPORTANCE OF HOW WE APPEAR TO OTHERS

> *'We awaken in others the same attitude of mind we hold toward them.'*
>
> —ELBERT HUBBARD

Self-assurance is fundamental for nurturing and projecting a positive attitude, yet the contrast between our inner feelings and how others perceive us can be striking. The difference in how people see us compared to our own self-view highlights the crucial necessity of aligning these divergent perspectives. It's a paradox worth exploring—what leads certain individuals to exude a sense of seriousness? What motivates them to derive visible satisfaction from displaying their status and power? Often, the root cause is insecurity. A lack of genuine confidence in their worth drives them to constantly showcase superiority and seek validation from others, masking their insecurities behind a façade of dominance.

Vanity adds another layer; the natural desire to feel significant can sometimes spiral into unchecked egotism, resulting in rather amusing exhibitions. Here's a light-hearted reminder, 'Only two groups of people believe flattery: men and women.' It serves as a gentle push to stay grounded, maintaining a balanced perspective without soaring too high in the realm of self-importance.

Superficiality can also prompt individuals to overstate their importance, blinding them to the bigger picture. This narrow focus often distorts their understanding, skewing their perception of their role and influence.

Individuals fostering a positive attitude often find themselves propelled into leadership roles, and it's not without reason. Their optimistic outlook equips them to confront challenges with greater agility, fostering a sense of accomplishment in professional endeavours and contentment in their personal lives. Such individuals naturally command respect and draw followers due to their infectious positivity. When entrusted with leadership, they wield their authority not to assert superiority but to steer towards desired goals, all while maintaining a belief in equality and recognizing the worth of those they lead.

There's a particular exasperation in witnessing someone, whether young or older, excessively consumed by their self-image. So, a gentle word of caution—should you feel yourself leaning towards either extreme, it's wise to tread carefully! Recognizing this tendency acts as a safeguard, preventing the descent into the pitfalls of taking oneself too seriously, regardless of age or stage in life. This awareness serves as a guiding beacon, keeping one grounded amid the lure of self-importance.

THE CHALLENGE OF LEADING

In a prior role, I had the chance to collaborate with a Senior Vice President who oversaw a thriving $350 million retail store chain. Their ambitious goal was to triple sales within five years. Eager to learn about the personal growth needed for such rapid expansion, I posed the question, 'What personal development do you envision in achieving this remarkable growth?' The Senior VP's reply was unexpected, to say the least, 'I don't dwell on that. Frankly, I never envisioned reaching this level. I have a lot of self-assurance, so the future doesn't unsettle me.'

This response revealed a reluctance toward introspection and self-assessment, essential components for fostering growth. Moreover, the lack of consideration for grooming potential successors indicated a disconnect from the evolving landscape. Despite a quarter-century of experience in that elevated role, there was a failure to grasp the fundamental truth that lasting change must start from within. Interestingly, his fellow executives didn't see him as promotable, underscoring the disparity between his perception and the collective sentiment.

There's a saying that goes, 'Ideas are not rare. Making them useful is.' This saying captures the essence of effective leadership. Whether managing a small-scale project or heading a corporate division, the ultimate goal remains constant: achieving specific objectives through the collaborative efforts of others. Despite its apparent simplicity, accomplishing this objective requires a series of demanding prerequisites and commitments.

Steering a collective toward defined goals in a leadership role involves much more than overseeing operations—it requires creating an environment that propels collective efforts toward a shared vision. This intricate task demands a delicate balance of strategic planning, effective communication, adept decision-making and the crucial ability to inspire and motivate team members.

To achieve objectives through others, a leader needs a diverse skill set that goes beyond technical proficiency. Emotional intelligence, building trust and instilling confidence are equally vital. It's an ongoing journey of growth, adaptation and evolution, where the primary focus is on aligning actions with desired outcomes while fostering a collaborative and cohesive team dynamic.

Whenever you're asked to lead, whether it is a small project or a corporate division, the objective is the same: to achieve specific goals through the efforts of others. No matter what methods you select, your major responsibility must be to provide leadership in achieving expected results. Although this may seem relatively simple, the requirements for making it happen are demanding.

KEY FACTORS INVOLVED IN LEADERSHIP

Creating an environment that fosters the full potential of individuals and teams stands as a crucial responsibility for leaders. Achieving this entails skillfully navigating several core aspects.

First and foremost, detailed planning serves as the foundation. However, the ability to adapt and improvise in the face of unforeseen circumstances is equally essential. Flexibility acts as the catalyst, allowing leaders to guide their teams through unknown territories, ensuring progress despite unexpected challenges.

Successful leadership involves a dual role: being an innovator and an executor. It requires introducing new ideas and processes while adeptly managing day-to-day operations crucial for sustaining the team's momentum. Balancing these roles showcases a leader's ability to maintain both forward motion and the stability necessary for sustainable growth.

Asking impactful questions serves as another crucial element. Leaders who pose thought-provoking queries stimulate critical thinking, encourage action and foster ongoing improvement within their teams. Well-crafted questions spark innovation and advancement.

Monitoring progress goes beyond mere observation; it involves orchestrating timely adjustments and recalibrations. Effective leaders consistently assess individual and group progress, swiftly implementing necessary changes and charting new courses of action to ensure alignment with overarching goals. This proactive approach guarantees that both individuals and plans stay on course in a continually evolving landscape.

Furthermore, the mastery of persuasion holds greater power than dominance. Vital to this skill is the mastery of effective communication. Actively listening and responding with clear, simple and empathetic articulation stands as the cornerstone. Instead of imposing personal viewpoints, successful leaders adeptly persuade and motivate through their actions, setting an example that empowers others to follow suit.

In short, effective leadership isn't a singular talent but rather a harmonious fusion of adaptability, innovation, inquiry, proactive supervision and persuasive communication. It involves orchestrating a symphony of actions that not only inspire and motivate but also guide individuals and teams toward shared goals, fostering continuous growth and development every step of the way.

WHAT EFFECTIVENESS REQUIRES

'Winners mix optimism with opportunity.'

In the contemporary business landscape, successful competitors show an unwavering commitment to self-improvement and continuous learning. They invest substantial time in delving into the intricacies of their organization—the structures, policies and goals—culminating in a profound understanding of their duties and areas of influence. Moreover, they possess a sharp insight into group dynamics and relationships, adeptly identifying avenues for personal growth and supervisory development within their domain.

Effective leadership isn't solely about gathering knowledge; it necessitates an intricate understanding of evolving trends and emerging patterns. Being static amidst rapid changes leads to lagging behind. Leaders who thrive amid intense competition exhibit distinct characteristics.

They excel in managing interpersonal dynamics, skillfully guiding teams to promote purposeful and cohesive organizational functioning. Their approach to problem-solving merges orderliness with empathy, showcasing thoughtfulness, tact and thoroughness. In their pursuit of peak performance, they consistently earn the respect and admiration of those around them.

Self-motivation is a defining trait—effective leaders adeptly manage themselves, constantly improving their skill sets and actively seeking new ideas and methodologies.

Moreover, their profound comprehension of the balance between efficiency and effectiveness sets them apart. While efficiency involves doing things correctly, effectiveness encompasses doing the right things accurately—balancing the pursuit of optimal outcomes with a focused emphasis on achieving results that genuinely matter.

Identifying critical areas for results and evaluating progress measures becomes imperative. Quick decision-making isn't the core; instead, the most adept competitors carefully plan actions after thorough consideration of what needs to be accomplished.

This intentional approach ensures deliberate actions aligned with overarching objectives.

Interestingly, a substantial number of individuals lack a clear understanding of their job expectations. A beneficial exercise to gauge performance priorities involves answering concisely, 'What am I paid to do?' Limiting each item to no more than four words, without directional cues or quantifiable metrics, offers a distilled yet comprehensive understanding of key goals.

Assessing these objectives against specific criteria is crucial. This involves verifying that they embody tangible output, align with one's responsibilities and authority, avoid duplications or gaps with other tasks and seamlessly integrate both vertically and horizontally within the team structure. This process acts as a litmus test, aligning personal objectives with the broader organizational goals and the overall team structure. This exercise plays a pivotal role in defining and fine-tuning performance priorities, aiding in strategic planning and ensuring a cohesive alignment with the organization's objectives.

ARE YOU AN EFFECTIVE LEADER?

'The greatest risk is to risk nothing.'

Peter Drucker's pioneering research introduced a distinct array of attributes that define effective leadership. These qualities, articulated by Drucker, persist in delineating genuine leadership.

Firstly, leaders kickstart projects by delving into the fundamental question, 'What needs to be accomplished?' This proactive stance highlights a leader's dedication to collective objectives and broader organizational goals, prioritizing these over individual needs or desires.

Continual introspection into an organization's overarching purposes and objectives is another hallmark of effective leadership. This ongoing examination aims for clarity on acceptable performance standards and contributions that tangibly enhance the organization's overall value. Such keen awareness ensures alignment with strategic objectives, enabling sustainable growth.

Additionally, true leaders refrain from creating replicas of themselves within their teams. They steer clear of subjective judgments driven by personal preferences, yet they are resolute in not accepting subpar performance. Their primary focus remains fostering a culture where performance takes precedence.

Another remarkable attribute of effective leaders is their lack of intimidation when others possess strengths they might lack themselves. Rather than feeling threatened, they harness the diverse strengths within their team, understanding that collective capabilities form a more resilient and adaptable unit.

Drucker's astute observations on leadership traits seamlessly align with a modern understanding of competitiveness. If we substitute 'leaders' with 'competitors' in Drucker's delineated qualities, a parallel becomes evident. Competitors, akin to effective leaders, initiate projects focusing on essential tasks, prioritizing collective goals over individual desires. Consistently assess their organization's goals and performances, ensuring alignment with strategic imperatives contributing to their competitive advantage. Avoid uniformity, prioritizing performance over personal preferences and cultivating a culture of excellence. Embrace diverse strengths within their competitive landscape, leveraging varied competencies to strengthen their own positions.

Drucker's perceptive insights transcend mere leadership paradigms, offering profound insights into competitiveness. They highlight the significance of collective objectives, performance-driven cultures and the strategic importance of diversity in achieving and sustaining a competitive edge across all domains.

CARING CANNOT BE FAKED

Authentic care cannot be mimicked; it's inherently genuine and cannot be fabricated. It's the bedrock of creating a positive environment. However, contemporary perspectives on care diverge widely. Some sceptics argue that genuine care is diminishing in today's society, while others suggest an overabundance of self-absorption.

The topic of caring remains complex, with unanswered questions even among social scientists. How and when do we develop the ability to care? Who takes on the role of caregivers? Does this sentiment have relevance in the business world? Can caring be taught?

Jack Beasley, a Professor of Family and Child Studies at Georgia Southern College and a consultant focusing on family issues, links caring to understanding others' perspectives and responding empathetically. He sees caring as a skill honed throughout life. Interestingly, techniques used to nurture children's capacity for care also enhance productivity and foster better professional relationships, even for adults.

To those seeking to elevate their caring capacities, Professor Beasley offers a set of foundational techniques to consider:

1. Start by observing how individuals respond in situations where their team faces adversity or encounters loss. Learning from these scenarios provides insights into the dynamics of care within a group setting.

2. Demonstrate authentic care consistently. Studies show that employees who perceive their leaders and colleagues as genuinely caring tend to exhibit higher levels of productivity and engagement.
3. Exercise discretion in your care. Knowing when to step back is a pivotal aspect of genuine concern. Tailor your support to individual needs without imposing excessive assistance that might diminish their autonomy or self-confidence.
4. Foster a space for individuals to learn from the consequences of their actions. While offering guidance and warnings is beneficial, firsthand experience often solidifies understanding and belief.
5. Maintain a delicate balance between caring for others and attending to your own needs. Care stems from a foundation of self-worth and esteem. Individuals secure in themselves are less likely to seek external validation, contrasting those grappling with self-identity issues. Encourage others to enhance their capabilities, empowering them to take credit for their personal growth.
6. Prioritize self-care. Contrary to being selfish, prioritizing your own well-being is fundamental. It's challenging to demonstrate genuine care for others without first attending to your own needs.

Adopting these techniques not only fosters an environment grounded in authentic concern but also reinforces productivity, nurtures relationships and cultivates personal development. These practices underscore the profound impact of genuine care in both personal and professional realms, resonating deeply with those seeking to foster holistic growth and meaningful connections.

Feigning care often leads to repercussions that circle back, causing adverse outcomes—a lesson encapsulated in Mark Twain's timeless wisdom, 'If you tell the truth, you don't have to remember anything.'

When insincerity taints your care for others, it rarely escapes notice. People have an innate ability to distinguish genuine concern from pretense. A lack of authentic care can foster demotivation and unhappiness among individuals. Conversely, when authentic care shapes your interactions, those around you take note and tend to reciprocate. This leads you to naturally:

- Challenge individuals with meaningful and purposeful work assignments.
- Acknowledge and appreciate their efforts by praising their achievements.
- Stand firmly behind decisions that affect their well-being.
- Pay attention to their genuine needs rather than imposing your assumptions.

For those in managerial roles or aiming for such positions, it's crucial to deeply reflect on why they seek leadership. Self-assessment regarding one's genuine interest in the team's welfare is paramount. If the assessment yields a 'No' or an uncertain 'I'm not sure', attempting to fake care will yield minimal benefits. Genuine care simply cannot be fabricated. To dispel any doubt, one can ask themselves, 'Among the pretenses I've encountered, who would I willingly follow?'

Honest evaluation of motivations for leadership forms the bedrock of genuine care and effective leadership. Trying to masquerade or feign care only perpetuates insincerity, ultimately hindering personal and team growth. This introspection serves as a compass, guiding leaders toward authentic care and fostering a culture of sincerity and growth within their teams.

3
HOW ATTITUDE AFFECTS RESULTS

*'I am not saying a Positive Attitude can make you successful.
I am saying a Positive Attitude will make you successful.'*

—NORMAN VINCENT PEALE

Understanding the crucial role a boss plays in one's job satisfaction and career development is of utmost importance. Whether working under an exceptional leader, mentor and guide, or facing challenges with a less-than-ideal supervisor, an individual's approach toward their manager significantly shapes their job experience.

Adapting and customizing actions to align with the boss's objectives, work style and practices can greatly enhance the working dynamic. A vivid example is Linda's experience in the Purchasing Department. Recognizing Carol's meticulous nature and preference for structured work, Linda consciously adjusted her approach. She keenly observed Carol's emphasis on punctuality and organizational skills, which contrasted with her previous boss's approach. Determined to adapt, Linda transformed her work habits by arriving earlier, meticulously organizing her workspace and modifying her attire to match a more conservative demeanour.

This proactive adaptation laid the groundwork for a successful relationship with Carol, fostering a productive and harmonious work environment. Linda's willingness to align her work practices with her supervisor's expectations not only cultivated a positive workplace atmosphere but also propelled her career advancement swiftly within the department. This instance emphasizes the significance of adapting to the supervisor's preferences, which can substantially impact professional growth and job satisfaction.

DOS AND DON'TS IN DEALING WITH YOUR BOSS

When navigating interactions with your supervisor, foundational guidelines play a crucial role in crafting effective coping mechanisms:

The Dos:

- Observe and learn from colleagues who maintain a positive rapport with your boss. Their strategies for managing workplace dynamics serve as invaluable examples to model and adopt.
- Consider the possibility that your role might contribute to any strain in your relationship with your supervisor. Acknowledge the shared responsibility in the situation—while you can't change your boss, modifying your behaviour can impact the dynamic. Take ownership and initiate actions to foster positive changes.
- Volunteer to take on tasks that your supervisor might not prefer, thereby helping to alleviate their workload and demonstrating your proactive approach.

- Stay attentive to your boss's mood patterns, noting when they appear more open and approachable during certain times of the day or week.
- Express your feelings about your boss's treatment, but choose an appropriate time—wait until your boss has calmed down and have a calm, private discussion about your concerns.
- Evaluate your progress regularly. If you're not seeing the desired results, reassess your approach to interacting with your supervisor. Adjust your strategy if needed, understanding that changes might take time to yield noticeable effects. Maintain patience and perseverance, knowing that progress often unfolds gradually.

The Don'ts:

- Avoid getting into disputes over your employer's authority, even if you have a differing viewpoint regarding their judgment in a specific scenario. Upholding their authority, especially during disagreements, helps maintain a professional demeanour within the workplace.
- Resist interpreting criticism as a personal attack. Distinguishing between your manageable job responsibilities and your boss's behaviour, which might not align with your expectations, can help maintain professional balance.
- Refrain from constantly seeking your boss' approval for every action. Taking initiative and carrying out tasks when necessary shows autonomy while keeping your boss informed afterward.

- Steer clear of engaging in gossip or negative discussions about your boss behind their back. Demonstrating loyalty and professionalism in all interactions fosters a respectful work environment.
- Avoid bypassing your boss's authority, except in urgent circumstances like emergencies. Disregarding the established chain of command often leads to complexities rather than resolving issues.
- Prioritize your self-respect above all else. If your coping strategies haven't been effective and a transfer isn't an option, preserving your self-esteem is crucial. If necessary, explore opportunities for a new job under a different supervisor to ensure your professional dignity and fulfilment.

Remember, forming definitive judgments about individuals should be based not solely on their words or intentions but on observed evidence and the actual outcomes of their actions and behaviour.

IDENTIFY ACCOUNTABLE PEOPLE

Evaluating the success of a business often reveals that financial insufficiency isn't the sole cause of failure. More often, it's the realization that wrong individuals have been engaged in pivotal roles that leads to setbacks. Assessing the dynamics within your professional circle—comprising your boss, colleagues and employees—becomes crucial in understanding their influence on your success trajectory.

While financial resources are undeniably vital, the people factor remains a linchpin in achieving business objectives.

The attitudes, skills and motivations of those around you significantly impact the overall efficacy of your efforts. Therefore, it's imperative to meticulously consider the roles played by each person within your professional network.

Your boss, for instance, holds a pivotal position in guiding your work environment and setting the tone for collaboration and productivity. Colleagues contribute to the collective synergy, potentially fostering innovation or, conversely, creating obstacles that hinder progress. Additionally, your employees significantly shape the execution of tasks and the attainment of goals.

Assessing whether these individuals align with your vision, provide constructive support and actively contribute to the collective success is crucial. Recognizing whether they empower or impede progress can help guide your decisions, ensuring a conducive environment for growth and success. Evaluating these dynamics allows for a comprehensive understanding of the people-related elements shaping the outcomes within your professional ecosystem.

THE LEAST VALUABLE PEOPLE (LVP) PROFILE

This checklist, referred to as my 'Least Valuable People' (LVP) profile, has emerged as a pivotal tool for discerning behavioural patterns that could either predict success or signal potential failure among individuals. It's an effective instrument for assessing personal attributes that hold significant weight in determining professional advancements or setbacks.

Its efficacy lies in its straightforward binary nature: Guilty or Not Guilty. This simplicity facilitates self-evaluation and the evaluation of others, making the process relatively accessible. Commencing with self-assessment allows for introspection before extending the evaluation to others.

What makes it particularly intriguing is how the listed traits serve as indicators of attitudes and behaviours that either drive someone towards success or impede their progress. For instance, avoiding problems, assigning blame for failures or missing deadlines could indicate a lack of accountability and initiative. Conversely, actively seeking clarification, taking calculated risks and nurturing talent are traits typically associated with successful individuals.

Through an analysis of these traits, individuals gain insights into their attitudes and approaches towards work. It enables them to distinguish between behaviours that contribute to success and those that lead to failure. This process of identifying these attributes serves as a catalyst for self-improvement and aids in making informed decisions about professional alignments and associations.

Start by rating yourself first as guilty or not guilty.

1. Constantly sidesteps problems and complaints, hoping someone else will handle them. _____
2. Avoids disciplining people. _____
3. Blames others when things go wrong. _____
4. Allows false statements to go unchallenged. _____
5. Doesn't worry about being late for work or meetings. _____
6. Postpones completion of projects as long as possible. _____
7. Avoids seeking clarification of misunderstandings in order to criticize later. _____
8. Never volunteers for an assignment when not absolutely certain of success. _____

9. Doesn't worry about deadlines. _____
10. Maintains the same sources of information and bases decisions more on opinions than facts. _____
11. Tries to be as noncommittal as possible. _____
12. Punishes good people who disagree. _____
13. Sees delegating as a way of getting rid of unpleasant chores rather than improving and expanding productivity. _____
14. Keeps busy on current projects and is uncomfortable about future planning. _____
15. Allows someone else to do recruiting and selection. _____
16. Tends to criticize others in public, rather than in private. _____
17. Is insulated from contact with customers. _____
18. Frequently talks about how much others depend on them. _____
19. Is not concerned about nurturing promotable people. _____
20. Is uncomfortable when depending on others to provide answers. _____
21. Concentrates efforts on favourite tasks rather than highest priorities. _____
22. Rarely compliments others for their good work. _____
23. Downplays the competence of other people. _____
24. Takes as few risks as possible. _____
25. Waits as long as possible before delivering bad news. _____
26. Limits efforts to 'on-the-job' hours; rarely takes work home. _____

27. Is not involved in self-improvement programs. _____

28. Joins in conversations about the 'good old days' as often as possible. _____

29. Talks a lot about how difficult it is to objectively measure what they do. _____

30. Hides talented people to further their own career. _____

Upon examining your responses, the frequency of 'Guilty' verdicts can unveil pivotal behavioural inclinations that could significantly influence either your or another individual's professional journey. Here's a comprehensive breakdown of the assessment based on the number of 'Guilty' verdicts:

0–4 Guilty verdicts: this range typically signals a commendable level of accountability and responsibility. Individuals falling within this scope are assets of considerable value. It's paramount to retain and cultivate their contributions within your team or organization.

5–10 Guilty verdicts: those within this category exhibit a mix of positive traits alongside certain areas of concern. With suitable guidance and support, they possess the potential to grow and handle more significant responsibilities. Mentorship and coaching can greatly aid their advancement.

11–20 Guilty verdicts: individuals with numerous 'Guilty' verdicts warrant careful observation. Their behaviours might present potential risks to your organization's efficiency and success. Vigilant monitoring and timely addressing of problematic aspects become imperative.

More than 20 Guilty verdicts: a high frequency of 'Guilty' verdicts signifies significant apprehensions in behaviour and attitude. Such individuals might pose severe challenges and risks to the organization. If you're in a supervisory role, documenting their problematic behaviour and seeking guidance from Human Resources is advisable. As a colleague, minimizing interactions could be beneficial. If this individual is your supervisor, maintaining professionalism while exploring a transfer might be a wise consideration.

Interpreting these outcomes equips you with valuable insights into the potential impact of individual behaviours. Armed with this understanding, informed decisions regarding collaboration, mentorship or addressing concerning patterns can be made proactively.

GET THE HELP YOU NEED

'Keep away from people who try to belittle your ambitions. Small people always do that, but the really great make you feel that you too can become great.'

—MARK TWAIN

Recognizing vulnerability in relying on others' performance stands as a defining trait of accomplished individuals. They grasp the significant influence that their surroundings—be it their team, colleagues or mentors—can wield over their own success. Creating a circle of individuals who uplift and complement one's abilities becomes a strategic move in fostering both personal and collective growth.

Leveraging insights from the LVP profile extends beyond flagging problematic situations; it's also about identifying the potential within those who exhibit exceptional qualities:

1. **Exceeding Expectations:** exceptional individuals refuse to settle after meeting baseline standards. They consistently aim for progress beyond existing benchmarks.
2. **Solution-Driven:** instead of simply highlighting problems, they propose solutions. Their approach is collaborative, framing challenges as collective issues and offering actionable recommendations.
3. **Resilience in Mistakes:** rather than shifting blame, they take ownership of errors and display resilience. They explore alternative approaches to rectify mistakes.
4. **Accountability Sans Excuses:** when things go awry, they take responsibility and focus on resolving the issue without resorting to excuses.
5. **Self-Management:** they proactively handle their tasks, establishing interim deadlines for long-term projects to eliminate last-minute panics.
6. **Pursuing Improvement:** prioritizing growth over perfection, they avoid falling into the trap of perfectionism that often leads to undue pressure and frustration, hindering actual progress.
7. **Foresight and Planning:** forward-thinking individuals anticipate challenges and proactively plan, reducing the likelihood of unpleasant surprises.
8. **Continuous Momentum:** they refrain from dwelling excessively on past successes or errors. Instead, they swiftly pivot from both triumphs and missteps, focusing on present tasks or future objectives. This forward momentum encourages an environment of continual improvement and growth.
9. **Curiosity:** they recognize the significance of seeking clarity. When faced with uncertainty, they actively seek

clarification, minimizing misunderstandings or errors.
10. **Proactive Decision-making**: successful individuals take a proactive stance in decision-making. They negotiate agreements and promptly initiate action aligned with agreed-upon terms, accelerating progress and fostering innovation within their roles.

In any organizational setting, those who take the lead, adeptly negotiate and willingly share their expertise stand as indispensable assets. These attributes—initiation, negotiation and teaching—play pivotal roles in propelling progress, resolving conflicts and nurturing development. Identifying, attracting and actively engaging individuals proficient in these areas greatly heightens the prospects of organizational triumph. Their capacity to instigate action, facilitate agreements and impart knowledge empowers teams, propelling the organization towards its objectives and fostering a culture rich in productivity and collaboration.

Spotting these qualities doesn't just help avoid potential pitfalls; it aids in establishing connections with individuals whose traits align with success-driven behaviours. Collaborating with such individuals elevates overall team performance and substantially contributes to the attainment of collective goals. Identifying and leveraging these strengths within the team amplifies its effectiveness and fortifies the path towards organizational success.

WHAT'S WRONG VS. WHO'S WRONG

It becomes imperative to deeply explore the intricacies of responsibility and mindset, particularly in the context of problem-solving and accountability within an organizational framework.

The difference between centring attention on what went wrong as opposed to who might be at fault represents a fundamental aspect of embracing a positive mindset and fostering accountability. A focus on 'who' tends to perpetuate a search for someone to hold responsible or blame when things don't go as planned. This perspective often creates an environment steeped in tension and defensiveness. In a culture driven by blame, team members become guarded, expecting accusations or finger-pointing, breeding an air of apprehension.

In contrast, centring on 'what' went wrong shifts the focus to understanding the issue itself. It involves a thorough analysis of the problem, pinpointing its origins and devising constructive remedies. This approach cultivates an environment where the emphasis lies on resolving issues rather than assigning blame. It encourages a collaborative culture where team members collectively tackle challenges without the fear of reprisal or fault-finding.

Thus, nurturing a workplace culture that promotes focusing on the problem rather than fixating on attributing blame to individuals becomes crucial. A culture that champions problem-solving and constructive dialogues over seeking fault fosters open and transparent communication. It instils a shared responsibility to surmount obstacles, propelling innovation, growth and nurturing a positive and productive work milieu.

ATTITUDE AND EFFECTIVENESS

> *'Success or failure in business is caused more by mental attitude than by mental capacities.'*
>
> —SIR WALTER SCOTT

Effectiveness in leadership roles intertwines closely with attitude, a facet often underestimated or overlooked. For supervisors, managers or leaders, their effectiveness hinges significantly on how their attitude impacts the outcomes achieved. Engaging in self-reflection and asking pivotal questions can shed light on how attitude molds leadership.

To gauge the influence of one's attitude on team success, delving into key inquiries proves insightful:.

1. Is there tangible evidence reflecting a genuine desire for the success of those under your leadership?
2. Does your conduct showcase a commitment to invest time in planning, foreseeing future needs and providing crucial resources for your team?
3. Can you maintain composure during crises, sidestepping impulsive reactions that might affect your team's response?
4. Do you cultivate an environment encouraging calculated risk-taking without penalizing bearers of unwelcome news?
5. How adeptly do you handle disagreements, preventing them from escalating into discordant interactions?
6. Do you refrain from exhibiting symbols of status or privilege that could instill fear, isolation or suspicion among team members?
7. Are you skilled in negotiating goals to be challenging yet achievable? Can you guide rather than dictate, coaching instead of imposing?
8. Are you seldom caught off-guard and possess the ability to swiftly obtain necessary information? While omniscience isn't essential, reducing surprises and knowing where to acquire pertinent information is pivotal.
9. Can you simplify complex issues, ensuring your

communication is easily understandable and minimizing the need for clarifications?
10. Do you foster dissenting opinions to arrive at more comprehensive decisions, acknowledging that unanimity might not always ensure a thorough examination, much like Alfred Sloan's practice?

Addressing these questions and actively adapting attitudes and behaviours based on the responses significantly shapes leadership effectiveness. The willingness to introspect and adjust attitudes creates an environment conducive to growth, innovation and overall success within the team or organization.

The inability to provide clear responses to these critical inquiries doesn't just highlight a lack of self-awareness but might also indicate a lack of transparency about how your attitudes influence the organization. When decision-makers assess your potential for career growth, they rely on tangible proof of how your attitudes shape your contributions.

It's crucial to align your attitudes with your daily conduct. Your actions serve as a visible reflection of your attitudes, painting a vivid picture of how you interact with tasks, colleagues and challenges. This harmony between your stated attitudes and your actual behaviours acts as a blueprint for others to grasp your approach, values and dedication to the organization's objectives. Therefore, ensuring that your attitudes consistently manifest in your actions plays a pivotal role in presenting a compelling case for career advancement.

OVERCOMING YOUR OWN NEGATIVE ATTITUDES

'The greatest discovery of my generation is that a human being can alter their life by altering attitudes.'

—WILLIAM JAMES

When realizing that one's actions or attitudes contribute to a problem, it presents an opportunity for personal development. Here are strategies to navigate such moments of self-awareness:

1. **Assess Negative Attitudes:** taking a pause to examine negative attitudes helps anticipate their potential consequences. By questioning, 'Where will this lead?' individuals gain insight into the outcomes of persisting with such attitudes.
2. **Embrace Humor:** laughter works as a potent remedy. Its ability to ease stress and lighten the atmosphere makes it an effective coping strategy during tough times.
3. **Embrace Setbacks Positively:** acknowledging setbacks as a natural part of life while maintaining a positive perspective can mitigate the impact and duration of problems.
4. **Practice Self-Encouragement:** engaging in calming self-talk in stressful moments can significantly reduce stress levels. Taking breaks, such as having lunch away from work, offers valuable moments to relax and recharge.
5. **Foster Positive Self-Talk:** when feeling down, encouraging oneself with positive affirmations can uplift mood and perspective.
6. **Evaluate Priorities and Goals:** assessing whether personal aspirations align with genuine desires or are influenced by external expectations is crucial. Authentic goal-setting is

vital for personal fulfillment.
7. **Simplify Matters:** streamlining decision-making by simplifying complexities where possible reduces unnecessary stress.
8. **Address Small Issues Early:** resolving minor problems promptly prevents them from escalating into larger, more complicated issues.
9. **Strengthen Social Bonds:** cultivating meaningful relationships with family and friends enriches life experiences. Nurturing these connections serves as a support system during tough times and requires as much dedication as one's professional role.
10. **Collaborative Problem-Solving:** brainstorming positive solutions with others fosters a constructive approach. Reflecting on alternative actions or words that could have resulted in a more positive outcome is a valuable exercise in growth and learning.

Embarking on a journey of change and growth entails facing a multitude of challenges. The process of apologizing, starting anew, admitting mistakes, persistently striving and accepting advice doesn't come without hurdles. These endeavours demand courage, humility and resilience as they involve not just recognizing personal flaws but also facing scepticism or disapproval from others.

Navigating the path of avoiding errors can be daunting, as some missteps may feel unavoidable despite our best efforts. Striving for sustained success brings its own difficulties; distractions often test our determination, making it tough to stay focused on the path to accomplishment.

Breaking free from harmful habits, avoiding stagnant

routines and embracing the liberating power of forgiveness demand significant effort. Exercising caution in our actions, managing our inner turbulence and taking responsibility for deserved blame are not endeavours for the faint-hearted.

While undeniably challenging, these endeavours act as stepping stones toward brighter futures, guiding us on a path of personal growth, fulfilment and ultimately, a more enriched life.

BUILD UP YOUR SELF-CONFIDENCE

'If you have a positive attitude and constantly strive to give your best effort, eventually you will overcome your immediate problems and find you are ready for greater challenges.'

—PAT RILEY

Mastering self-belief stands as a cornerstone in cultivating confidence, a quality that influences every facet of our existence. The attitude we project acts as a multidimensional reflection, vividly portraying our self-assuredness.

Boosting confidence necessitates addressing critical elements. Firstly, recognizing our limitations lays the groundwork for personal development. Secondly, refining the art of decision-making significantly contributes to self-assurance. Deepening our understanding of these vital components constructs a sturdy foundation for establishing and fostering self-belief.

WHAT LIMITATIONS WILL YOU ACCEPT?

In the 1960s, Jimmy Heuga stood as a dominant force in the skiing realm, showcasing his skill by securing a bronze medal in the 1964 Olympic slalom. However, at the age of twenty-five, disappointment clouded his spirits when he landed in eighth place in the same event in 1968. Little did he know, he was wrestling with the onset of multiple sclerosis, a diagnosis that hit him like a devastating blow.

Faced with grim predictions from multiple doctors who believed his nerve damage would confine him to a wheelchair, Heuga adamantly refused to accept their prognosis. Instead, he embarked on an unwavering journey to challenge the limitations imposed by his condition. Rejecting a state of helplessness, he adopted a rigorous routine, commuting on his bicycle, engaging in daily exercises and swimming for twenty minutes, demonstrating an unwavering determination. Furthermore, he took on the formidable challenge of relearning how to ski despite the obstacles presented by his illness.

His fundamental belief revolved around the idea that despite the potential confinement of a wheelchair, the concept of idleness and dependence was unimaginable. His focus centred on rejuvenating his life through a robust regimen for health. His core philosophy reverberates profoundly: circumvent the obstacles imposed by the disease. He likened this approach to learning to swim, where the initial stages involve simply getting one's feet wet, progressively wading deeper each day until confidence in swimming is achieved.

This mindset not only empowered Heuga to confront and manage his illness but also inspired him to establish the Heuga Center. This organization offers programs crafted from his personal journey to aid others grappling with MS, standing as a symbol of hope and resilience.

Truly, his narrative and methodology provide invaluable guidance to individuals navigating adversities, emphasizing the significance of resilience, persistence and adaptability in the face of challenges.

WHAT CHOICES DO YOU MAKE?

Ann Weber, a psychologist based in Asheville, North Carolina, sheds light on the inherent discomfort associated with decision-making, attributing it to the weighty responsibility that choices carry. She astutely observes the allure of indecision, a seemingly safe refuge where blame finds no foothold. However, she underscores the perilous downside of this approach: a life that spins beyond one's control.

Delving deeper into the intricate complexities of indecisiveness, Jane Burka, a psychologist from Berkeley, California, outlines various personality types grappling with decisiveness. Perfectionists, wary of making mistakes, opt to evade decisions rather than risk any potential error. Non-compromisers pursue the unattainable, feeling compromised at the slightest hint of concession. Freedom lovers, faced with an abundance of choices, recoil from commitment, continuously seeking open-ended possibilities. Then there are the dependents, who place greater trust in others' judgment than in their own.

What unites these disparate personas, as you might anticipate, is a common undercurrent of low self-esteem, often intricately tied to their upbringing. For instance, the perfectionist might emerge from a family environment where errors were met with harsh criticism. Dependents, too, might have been conditioned by constant admonitions about their decision-making abilities, ultimately leading to resignation.

Mike Hernacki, a writer hailing from San Diego, shares a similar sentiment, tracing his own lack of self-assurance and subsequent indecision back to his demanding upbringing. His childhood was entrenched in a stringent ethos, where praise was a rarity, and any achievement seemed to fall short of an unattainable perfection. He recalls moments of receiving excellent grades, only to be met with his father's dismissive comment of, 'What's with the B?'

Reflecting on a significant turning point in his life, Hernacki recounts a time when, despite being in a long-term relationship for four years, he struggled to gather the courage to propose until his partner issued an ultimatum. His career path navigated various trajectories, encompassing teaching, advertising, law and stockbroking. However, his dream of becoming a writer lay dormant for fourteen years due to his fixation on monetary success, believing that his prior professions failed to yield substantial income.

In a parallel journey, Frank McCourt's transition from Ireland to the United States was fraught with challenges. Arriving with no money, skills or companionship, he laboured through menial and exhausting jobs to finance his college education. Despite harbouring a deep desire to write, McCourt found himself teaching English in high schools in New York City. It wasn't until retirement that he finally found the confidence to pursue his writing aspirations. His debut book, *Angela's Ashes*, not only became a bestseller but also paved the way for two more critically acclaimed memoirs.

Psychologists Meryle Gillman and Diane Gage, authors of *The Confidence Quotient: 10 Steps to Conquer Self-Doubt*, advise those struggling with indecision to examine negative influences that have shaped their perspectives. They propose an exercise where individuals visualize their doubters, like a critical parent, alongside a supportive figure. This mental practice aims to reshape internal dialogue, creating a positive partnership between doubt and encouragement. The act of decision-making becomes pivotal, showing that life doesn't collapse regardless of outcomes, ultimately empowering a sense of control.

These examples underscore how upbringing significantly impacts confidence and decisiveness. They highlight childhood environments' crucial role in shaping self-perception and decision-making approaches, stressing the need for environments that foster self-worth and encourage making choices without fear of judgment.

Becoming more decisive involves actively participating in daily decision-making. Waiting for absolute control before deciding is like delaying quitting smoking until it becomes unbearable—an elusive scenario. Instead, making a series of small decisions lays the groundwork for decisiveness. It involves setting a course of action and following through, akin to saying, 'I'll take steps to quit smoking,' and committing to it.

Indecisiveness often stems from anxiety about an uncertain future. Yet, taking action often lessens the perceived dread of these uncertainties. The strategy involves breaking decisions into manageable steps. For example, in personal investments, one needn't dive into the entire stock market; focusing on essential knowledge about specific investments is a more approachable tactic.

Mike Hernacki's perspective is particularly resonant here. He emphasizes that the significance of decisions lies more in the commitment behind them than their immediate impact. He suggests that the majority of decisions aren't as pivotal as imagined, and very few are truly fatal. What matters is the dedication to making them work.

Hernacki admits that decision-making isn't always easy,

even now. However, he highlights the transformative power of a history of decisions, which builds confidence. This evolution signifies a shift in mindset—from hesitation to a resolute approach to decision-making.

Ultimately, this approach emphasizes the importance of a proactive stance in decision-making. It's about recognizing that the weight of decisions often lies in our commitment to seeing them through, and that consistent incremental steps lay the foundation for a more confident and empowered approach to life's choices.

> *'A positive attitude allows us to focus not on uncontrollable events but on how we respond to them.'*

4

MAXIMIZING YOUR PERFORMANCE

'For success, attitude is equally as important as ability.'

—HARRY F. BANKS

Attitude determines behaviour. The first question addressing this issue is, are you accountable?

ACCEPT RESPONSIBILITY FOR YOUR ACTIONS

Peter Drucker's insights into effective executive qualities hold substantial relevance in today's ever-evolving organizational settings. He emphasizes the importance of character development, foresight, self-reliance and courage among leaders. Drucker keenly notes that organizations consist of ordinary individuals tasked with accomplishing extraordinary goals. Yet, achieving these aspirations becomes unattainable if individuals evade accountability.

Instilling accountability becomes crucial. While taking responsibility might present challenges, avoiding it due to a fear of making mistakes signifies a failure in itself. Long-term success relies on the willingness to step up to leadership when necessary, even if it entails the risk of failure.

Perfect judgment eludes every person. The imperfections in human judgment are vividly portrayed in a story involving a woman who rose to a significant marketing role. In her initial assignment, she unintentionally made a severe mistake that resulted in a project failure, costing the company over $100,000. When summoned by her boss, she anticipated termination. Surprisingly, her boss responded, 'Fire you? No way. I just invested $100,000 in your training.'

This story poignantly illustrates the inherent fallibility in human decision-making. It emphasizes the critical nature of acknowledging and learning from mistakes rather than punishing individuals for their missteps. Such incidents often serve as pivotal learning moments, fostering personal growth and development.

Promoting a culture that nurtures accountability rather than penalizing it helps foster a resilient workforce. It allows individuals to take measured risks, encouraging innovation and learning from setbacks. Ultimately, embracing accountability not only cultivates a supportive environment but also drives organizational growth by transforming setbacks into valuable learning opportunities.

THINK BEFORE YOU DECIDE

Developing and honing judgment is a continuous journey rooted in thoughtfully considering key elements before making decisions. Embracing these principles can enhance your decision-making capabilities:

- Pause and reflect: rather than acting impulsively when confronted with a challenge, take the time to

methodically analyse the situation, aiming to anticipate potential outcomes.
- Assess all angles: for each possible solution, meticulously weigh its advantages, disadvantages, costs, risks and potential objections that might arise.
- Embrace objectivity: scrutinize facts without letting preconceptions cloud your judgment, as ignoring facts can lead to potential pitfalls.
- Mitigate biases and preferences: keep personal biases aside and consider others' perspectives. Reflect on how your decisions might affect colleagues or associates, recognizing that differing viewpoints can impact the success of plans.
- Embrace critique: recognize and value criticism as a vital aspect of the decision-making process.

Following these principles refines judgment, enabling more informed and considerate decision-making. Incorporating these practices not only strengthens decision-making abilities but also promotes an environment of inclusive and thoughtful problem-solving.

EXPECT PROBLEMS

In the realm of management, a prevalent deficiency surfaces—managers often shy away from tackling problems head-on, opting instead to dodge them. Their reluctance to confront issues arises from a fear of potential criticism and the misconception that avoiding decisions shields them from accusations of poor judgment.

However, a distinguished president of a prominent

corporation, renowned for nurturing associates' growth, approaches errors in judgment uniquely. His standard response to such situations echoes a resolute, 'All right, that's behind us; now what's our next move?' This approach signifies his emphasis on propelling forward momentum, urging individuals to take action and managers to adeptly lead. His underlying philosophy prioritizes action and values consistent achievement over the paralysis caused by the fear of making mistakes. Remarkably, this approach often yields the desired outcomes.

In essence, this method underscores a fundamental truth: life mirrors a batting average more than a perfect scorecard. It recognizes that imperfection is an inherent part of the journey towards progress and success. Embracing this philosophy nurtures an environment that esteems decisiveness, views mistakes as opportunities for learning and prioritizes moving forward over the dread of errors. Such an approach often sparks a culture of ongoing improvement, enabling organizations to adapt and flourish despite challenges.

> 'What happens to us is less important
> than what we make happen.'

PERCEPTION CAN BE REALITY

When it comes to workplace dynamics, effective communication stands as a cornerstone, regardless of your position within the organizational hierarchy. It's not just about the content of your message; it's equally about the tone and manner in which you convey it. The attitude you project toward your colleagues and employees echoes loudly throughout the workspace. Often, there's a curiosity surrounding directives—employees might ponder, 'Is this task meaningful, or just busywork? Am I being dumped with unfinished business from my boss? Will my effort contribute in a meaningful way?'

The way you assign tasks can significantly shape how your instructions are perceived. Simply dishing out orders without providing the 'why' behind them can lead to misunderstandings and a dip in morale. Thus, it's crucial to articulate not just the 'what' but also the 'why' when delegating responsibilities. Despite the temptation of straightforward commands, offering explanations is an invaluable practice.

By elucidating the rationale behind your requests, you transcend the label of being just bossy. You transform directives into logical and reasonable requests by providing a compelling reason for the task, fostering a more collaborative and understanding atmosphere.

Moreover, communicating the 'why' behind tasks acts as a proactive measure against errors. When individuals grasp the purpose clearly, they're less prone to mistakes. Additionally, in dynamic situations where circumstances change, this understanding empowers them to adapt and communicate back if the original action becomes obsolete.

Neglecting to offer sufficient context might lead to misunderstandings or blind adherence to instructions, fostering a culture where people execute orders without engaging their critical thinking skills. This lack of explanation might inadvertently create a scenario where errors are blamed on miscommunication rather than open and constructive dialogue.

By explaining the reasoning behind tasks, you instill trust and respect in your team members. It highlights the importance you place on clarity and background insights, encouraging them to tap into their analytical abilities. It's not just about relaying instructions; it's about nurturing an environment where individuals feel valued and empowered to offer suggestions, thereby making meaningful contributions to the task at hand.

Granted, there are times when explanations might seem obvious or urgent, necessitating immediate action. However, as a guiding principle, providing context and explanations remains a fundamental aspect of effective leadership and collaboration. It helps cultivate a culture of mutual understanding and enhanced productivity in the workplace.

KNOW YOUR COLLEAGUES

In-depth scrutiny of triumphant figures in the business domain often exposes the presence of four pivotal elements:

1. **Thoughtful Action:** those who thrive exhibit a penchant for pondering and evaluating before taking action or making decisions.
2. **Inner Drive:** they harbour an intrinsic motivation that propels them, fueling their pursuits with unwavering determination and perseverance.
3. **Embrace of Responsibility:** successful individuals willingly shoulder accountability, showcasing ownership of their actions and decisions.
4. **Leadership Proficiency:** they demonstrate the capacity to motivate and lead, acknowledging and leveraging team talents to realize collective objectives.

Within the ever-evolving landscape of organizations, individuals undergo transformations—some ascend while others stall, succumbing to complacency and apathy. An effective leadership challenge involves staying attuned to these shifts, recognizing and nurturing employees' budding talents even amid changing circumstances.

Long-standing employees, dedicated to their roles for extended periods, might inadvertently fade into the background due to their consistent reliability. However, their potential for growth and capability could surpass their current roles. Many have outgrown their positions and await opportunities for expansion and advancement.

One often overlooked aspect is the need for organizations to periodically reassess their employees. Even those seemingly settled might harbour untapped potential or be ready for greater challenges. The pitfall of pigeonholing individuals into roles they've outgrown is detrimental to both personal growth and the company's advancement.

While prioritizing workload remains crucial, identifying avenues to offer additional challenges to capable individuals is equally vital. For high performers, exploring opportunities for diversification is key. Can their skill set be tested with new responsibilities? Can they expand their expertise by tackling fresh challenges within their specialization?

Employers should avoid underestimating their employees' potential. Envisioning individuals thriving in more demanding scenarios is crucial. Past capabilities matter, but equally important is their present and future potential.

A telling illustration is H. Ross Perot's stint with GM. Perot, a successful innovator, was engaged by GM when their market share was dwindling. Despite his insights and track record, GM's entrenched management hesitated to embrace new perspectives, leading to missed opportunities. The clash between innovation and resistance to change resulted in a bias for maintaining the status quo.

This narrative emphasizes the significance of acknowledging fresh viewpoints and growth potential within an organization. Embracing change and fostering a culture open to new ideas often pave the way for sustained progress and success.

> *'Encourage your associates to express their ideas, especially when they differ from yours. Their disagreements not only provide you with new ideas, but give your insight into the way they approach problems that will help you work more effectively with them.'*
>
> —FRANKLIN C. ASHBY

POSITIVE ATTITUDE ENCOURAGES IMPROVED PERFORMANCE

Let's dive deeper into the significant impact of attitude on workplace productivity and explore the diverse facets of effective managerial practices that drive success.

The prevailing attitude within a workplace holds a substantial influence, extending beyond morale, self-esteem and behaviour—it directly intersects with the company's financial success. As a manager, your role transcends mere supervision; it involves cultivating an environment that optimizes employee productivity. Here are foundational suggestions to achieve this:

1. **Advocacy for Innovation:** serve as a conduit, transmitting progressive suggestions and innovative ideas from team members to upper management. Encourage a culture that values and recognizes fresh thinking.

2. **Nurturing Creativity:** cultivate an environment where creative thought is nurtured, ensuring individuals feel secure to share novel ideas without fear of ridicule or criticism. Creativity thrives in an atmosphere of acceptance and open-mindedness.
3. **Acknowledgment of Contributions:** credit the originators of ideas. By recognizing individuals for their contributions instead of claiming their ideas as your own, you not only honour their efforts but also inspire more innovative solutions.
4. **Purposeful Task Assignments:** assign tasks that employees find meaningful and impactful. The sense of accomplishment derived from substantial assignments that contribute tangibly to company growth can serve as a powerful motivator.
5. **Fostering a Sense of Belonging:** aid employees in understanding the unique aspects of being part of your organization. Creating a sense of belonging can cultivate stronger bonds and commitment among team members.
6. **Highlighting Significance:** encourage reflection on the importance of the team's work. Sometimes, employees undervalue their contributions due to a lack of recognition or acknowledgment.
7. **Beyond Monetary Compensation:** while financial rewards are crucial, acknowledge that employees seek more than just money. Participation, recognition, a sense of belonging and opportunities for achievement hold significant weight. When these aspects are fostered within a fair compensation framework, the sole pursuit of money diminishes.

By implementing these strategies, managers can create an

environment where employees feel valued, recognized and find purpose in their work. This holistic approach contributes to a more engaged and motivated workforce, significantly impacting the overall success of the organization.

> *'Ability is what you're capable of doing.*
> *Motivation determines what you do. Attitude*
> *determines how well you do it.'*
>
> —LOU HOLTZ

THE GENERATION GAP

Understanding the distinctive work attitudes among various generations, as unveiled by Professor Quinn Mills's extensive research at Harvard University, offers valuable insights into workplace dynamics. While factors like ethnic backgrounds and job sectors appear to have minimal impact on values, age disparities significantly mold workplace perceptions and behaviours.

1. **Authority Acceptance:** the aftermath of World War II shaped the older generation, fostering a tendency to respect and embrace authority figures. Conversely, the 'baby boomers', emblematic of the younger generation raised during the Vietnam era, tend to exhibit skepticism towards authority, showing a general lack of trust.
2. **Perception of Work:** a stark contrast in work ethos exists between generations. The older cohort considers work as a solemn duty, essential for self and family support. In contrast, the younger generation views work as an arena

for social interaction, enjoyment and fun, positioning it as a pivotal social space akin to recreational areas like health clubs.
3. **Promotion and Performance:** perspectives on career advancement diverge significantly. The older generation regards experience as the key pathway to advancement, willing to invest time in apprenticeships with the expectation of future rewards. Conversely, the younger generation seeks swift progress based on their performance, questioning the necessity of waiting periods.
4. **Communication Styles:** observable differences emerge in communication styles. The older generation values tact in communication, while the younger generation prioritizes honesty and directness, perceiving tact as an avoidance tactic rather than a diplomatic approach.
5. **Fairness and Individuality:** while the older generation associates fairness with treating everyone equally, the younger generation advocates for fairness by embracing individuality and recognizing differences among individuals.
6. **Value Focus:** the older generation tends to prioritize possessions and status as symbols of success, while the younger generation values experiences and personal fulfillment over material possessions.

These nuanced differences underscore the complexity of generational attitudes in the workplace. Recognizing and embracing these variations can facilitate a more inclusive and understanding work environment, fostering collaboration and synergy among diverse generations, ultimately benefiting the organization's overall performance and culture.

Understanding and acknowledging generational disparities

in work attitudes holds the key to creating a harmonious and highly productive work environment. Managers and employers armed with this knowledge can use it as a tool to bridge gaps, foster collaboration and adapt work structures, thereby enhancing overall workplace satisfaction and performance.

The evolving landscape of generational dynamics in the workplace demands attention, particularly with the shift from the WWII generation to the baby boomer cohort, which now occupies pivotal managerial roles. As subsequent generations like Gen-X and Gen-Y, along with their children and grandchildren, enter the workforce, there's a noticeable shift in perspectives and values. These newer cohorts often exhibit independent thinking and a resistance to traditional authority structures.

Managers of today must immerse themselves in understanding the distinct expectations and attitudes of these younger generations to effectively engage and manage them. This understanding becomes increasingly crucial as the number of younger individuals in the workforce decreases, potentially leading to labour shortages and emphasizing the importance of addressing generational differences.

Surprisingly, there are hidden advantages in the inexperience of younger recruits, contrary to prevailing scepticism. Patrick Kelly and Bill Riddell from Physician Sales and Services, Inc., recognize the potential in leveraging this inexperience. They believe that assigning routine tasks to inexperienced individuals can infuse remarkable enthusiasm, provided there's a clear plan for their growth and advancement within the organization.

This strategy recognizes that individuals new to the industry, free from entrenched practices or preconceptions, might approach routine tasks with an unprecedented vigour and an open-minded outlook. The crucial element here is to pave a clear path for their professional development, align their roles with growth opportunities and foster an environment that appreciates their contribution, irrespective of their limited experience within the industry.

Harnessing the potential of inexperienced individuals by nurturing their enthusiasm and abilities can serve as a highly effective strategy, especially in transforming routine tasks into engaging avenues for growth and skill development. This not only revitalizes typical roles but also cultivates a culture that actively encourages progress and evolution, benefiting both the organization and the individuals involved.

Recruiting inexperienced individuals often opens doors for fresh perspectives and an influx of enthusiasm within the workforce. Leaders like Riddell are adept at recognizing and leveraging the potential of young talent. Riddell's method involves convincing these individuals that their current roles are transitional, with the expectation of transitioning to more significant responsibilities in a short span, sometimes as quickly as six months. This approach brings forth highly motivated team members willing to undertake various tasks, from driving delivery vans to performing janitorial duties.

Moreover, Riddell stresses the importance of embedding a distinctive company culture among recruits, particularly those arriving with previous experiences from other organizations. Many such individuals, having imbibed diverse workplace attitudes, need to 'unlearn' certain habits or approaches to fully embrace the ethos of their new workplace. It's about fostering a culture that aligns closely with the company's values and vision, which might occasionally require reorienting seasoned professionals.

Riddell has observed that bringing inexperienced individuals into the fold significantly aids in disseminating and assimilating the company culture more efficiently. Experienced hires, when surrounded by less experienced colleagues, find themselves in an environment that accelerates the cultivation of the desired work culture, aligning it more rapidly with the company's overarching goals and values.

Enterprise Rent-a-Car adopts a comparable philosophy in its recruitment approach. The company annually hires numerous management trainees from diverse global campuses. These recruits typically start from the bottom, performing tasks like car washing and customer pickups. However, those who excel in these seemingly mundane roles do so with enthusiasm because they recognize the potential for rapid career advancement within the organization.

This model, mirrored in Riddell's approach and Enterprise Rent-a-Car's recruitment philosophy, showcases how embracing inexperienced talent and nurturing them within the company culture can invigorate the workforce while paving the way for swift career progression. It underscores the importance of providing growth and development opportunities, regardless of the entry-level nature of initial tasks, ultimately fostering a culture of upward mobility and ambition within the organization.

'He who would accomplish little must sacrifice little. He who would accomplish much must sacrifice much.'

—JAMES ALLEN

5

SHARPENING YOUR INTERPERSONAL SKILLS

A positive attitude is undeniably transformative when navigating various options, yet the workplace frequently grapples not with technical deficiencies, but rather the absence of essential interpersonal skills. How colleagues interact can decisively shape the trajectory of success or failure within an organization. Surprisingly, many seemingly intricate workplace predicaments find resolutions in straightforward yet impactful actions.

The cornerstone of a harmonious workplace resides in consideration for others. It's showcased in punctuality, honouring designated meal and break times, minimizing personal interruptions, leaving individual matters outside the workspace, showing regard for others' possessions, adhering to dress codes, maintaining confidentiality and steering clear of detrimental office gossip. These ostensibly rudimentary behaviours, when practiced collectively, significantly mould a conducive work environment.

Additionally, proactive communication regarding potential areas of concern, long before they snowball into insurmountable issues, is of paramount importance. Addressing problems at their inception circumvents allowing minor grievances to escalate into catastrophic crises that become arduous to rectify.

Seizing the initiative represents another pivotal aspect. While respecting hierarchical structures remains imperative, offering assistance or support to colleagues when suitable cultivates a collaborative atmosphere. This demonstrates a willingness to transcend predefined boundaries to positively contribute to the team's success.

In essence, these apparently simple actions—manifesting consideration, proactive communication and seizing initiative—serve as the linchpin for effective workplace interactions. They not only underpin a harmonious environment but also curtail potential conflicts while nurturing a culture rooted in mutual respect and collaboration. Embracing these principles not only elevates individual relationships but also significantly bolsters the collective success of the organization.

'Pretend that every single person you meet has a sign around his or her neck that says MAKE ME FEEL IMPORTANT. Not only will you succeed in sales, you will succeed in life.'

—MARY KAYE ASH

PREPARING FOR CHANGE

The intrinsic connection between progress and change underscores the pivotal role of attitude in navigating transitions. Change, in all honesty, seldom arrives with comfort. Its arrival tends to evoke feelings of uncertainty and unease, prompting a natural inclination to question the virtues of maintaining the status quo. Despite this initial reluctance, the imperative of embracing new ideas remains indispensable for organizations aiming to remain competitive and innovative.

Strategies are instrumental in easing the unsettling waves of change.

Embracing Change: the introduction of change is most effective when done gradually. Presenting new ideas not as radical departures but as potential options tethered to successful past practices allows for thoughtful consideration before full implementation.

Nurturing Acceptance: gently highlighting the added benefits of new concepts without applying undue pressure nurtures open discussions. It's crucial to respect diverse opinions and consider implementing changes in smaller increments over time, fostering a more receptive atmosphere.

Handling Resistance: in the face of significant pushback, temporarily easing off the implementation might be a prudent move. Rather than abandoning the idea entirely, reframing or reintroducing it at a more opportune time or under different circumstances can bolster acceptance. Genuine support for change often proves more influential than logical arguments.

Preparing for Change: acknowledging the intricacies and challenges change poses is vital. Cultivating a positive outlook toward change aids personal adaptation and influences others, facilitating a smoother transition into new operational methods.

Navigating change extends beyond embracing new ideas; it's about cultivating an environment where change is seen as an opportunity, not a menace. This positive perspective plays a pivotal role in shaping how change is perceived and embraced throughout the workplace, fostering a culture where innovation and adaptability thrive.

OVERCOMING RESISTANCE TO CHANGE

Resistance to change in a workplace often reveals itself through various observable behaviours, offering clear indicators of potential challenges. These signs include increased absenteeism, higher turnover rates, a surge in transfer requests, a rise in complaints, reduced cooperation among team members, reluctance toward supporting new systems and an overall decrease in productivity.

These visible forms of resistance typically stem from changes that might evoke concerns about job security, the devaluation of individual skills or a reduction in compensation. These apprehensions regarding personal consequences serve as significant drivers for resistance against embracing new initiatives or any modifications to the established organizational structure.

To garner sustained support for new ideas or changes, two fundamental approaches stand out: firstly, cultivating an environment that fosters active involvement and participation, and secondly, proactively addressing and mitigating brewing sentiments of resentment. These strategic methods not only facilitate the introduction of change but also ensure its smooth assimilation within the workplace culture. This, in turn, leads to a higher level of acceptance and successful integration of new practices or alterations.

ENCOURAGE PARTICIPATION

Acknowledging and addressing the persistent issues within a work environment stands as a critical initial step toward achieving meaningful progress. By actively pinpointing these ongoing challenges, a clearer comprehension of their root causes emerges, empowering a more targeted and effective approach to resolving them. Taking action upon identifying these concerns becomes pivotal to institute necessary changes.

In the pursuit of problem-solving or managing routine tasks, actively soliciting suggestions plays a vital role in attaining ultimate success. Esteemed leaders recognize the inherent value in the insights and innovative ideas possessed by most individuals. However, the lack of employee suggestions often stems from an environment where their input isn't actively sought or appreciated by their managers. This absence of encouragement stifles the generation of novel and more effective approaches to tasks or problems.

Tapping into the wealth of knowledge and experiences held by those directly involved in day-to-day operations becomes imperative. With a nudge of encouragement, individuals can offer invaluable suggestions for improvement. Astute leaders comprehend that frontline staff, engaged in the daily execution of tasks, often harbour the most innovative ideas for enhancing processes or operations.

The effectiveness of leaders isn't solely gauged by their individual performance but also by the collective efforts of their team. Managers who cultivate an environment that encourages innovation and idea-sharing tend to unlock their team's full potential, igniting progress and fostering growth within the organization. This approach not only harnesses the collective intelligence but also nurtures a culture that embraces continuous improvement.

It's evident that astute managers are often paired with proficient assistants, not merely by chance but through intentional efforts to develop them. Encouraging critical thinking and nurturing a sense of responsibility among team members sets the stage for both individual and collective growth.

A fundamental yet highly effective approach to stimulate a stream of suggestions is by actively seeking them out. Engaging those involved in discussions about prevailing problems or challenges often results in a wealth of innovative ideas and potential solutions. Embracing and valuing these contributions not only cultivates an atmosphere of collaboration but also empowers individuals within the team.

Moreover, expressing gratitude for the suggestions received and taking time for thoughtful consideration before responding goes a long way. This not only acknowledges the efforts of contributors but also demonstrates a sincere commitment to assessing and potentially implementing viable ideas. It's a testament to the value placed on the input received and the willingness to explore feasible solutions.

REJECTING SUGGESTIONS WITHOUT CAUSING RESENTMENT

During a team meeting led by Margo Marston to tackle an issue, Diane, a new team member, offered a potential solution. However, Margo's immediate response, based on previous unsuccessful attempts at a similar idea, was a blunt dismissal, 'We tried that before and it didn't work.' While this response reflected the reality of past challenges, Diane perceived it as a rejection of her suggestion, leaving her disheartened. This experience led her to feel a sense of resentment and reluctance in sharing future ideas, fearing they'd meet the same instant dismissal.

Considering this situation, how could Margo have handled Diane's suggestion differently to avoid causing such a negative impact?

One approach involves handling such rejections privately rather than in a group setting. Instead of an immediate dismissal, Margo could have thanked Diane for her contribution and expressed the intention to review it further. Later, in a one-on-one conversation, Margo could have delicately addressed the prior unsuccessful attempt by explaining, 'We had serious problems with it.' This approach leaves room for further discussion and potential improvements. This way, Diane might have responded differently, possibly acknowledging overlooked aspects or proposing modifications to address previous issues.

Another effective tactic involves using probing questions, akin to Socrates' teaching style. Margo could have guided Diane's thought process by asking relevant questions. Well-phrased inquiries could have prompted Diane to re-evaluate her initial idea, encouraging her to refine it into a more workable solution.

When declining suggestions, a gentle approach is essential. It's crucial to express genuine appreciation for the ideas while emphasizing the desire for more contributions. This attitude nurtures an environment where individuals feel valued and motivated to continue sharing, fostering the belief that their next idea could be the breakthrough solution.

> *'Give thanks and celebrate a positive attitude.*
> *It enables you to test your potential every day.'*

6

CONQUERING BURNOUT AND STRESS

'Expect trouble as an inevitable part of life and when it comes, hold your head high, look it squarely in the eye and say, "I will be bigger than you. You cannot defeat me."'

—ANN LANDERS

Every profession, with its unique demands and challenges, inherently carries its own dose of stress. In fact, a certain level of stress is deemed vital to sustain engagement and productivity; it injects a much-needed sense of challenge that prevents the stagnation of routine and monotony from settling in. However, it's at the tipping point where stress transitions into distress that pervasive issues begin to surface. This critical juncture often becomes evident through pronounced behavioural shifts.

Individuals renowned for their unwavering patience might, at this juncture, suddenly exhibit surprising signs of impatience. Normally composed and collected individuals might unexpectedly display visible tension or agitation. Employees, once highly cooperative and aligned with organizational goals, might exhibit subtle or overt rebellious tendencies, challenging established norms or authority. Others may endure physical manifestations, expressing difficulty in falling asleep or maintaining a restful night's sleep. Even after what appears to be a rejuvenating rest, they might persistently battle fatigue, experiencing physical discomfort such as stomach disturbances, a racing heart or frequent headaches.

While physical rest can alleviate bodily fatigue to some extent, the enduring persistence of mental fatigue remains a prevalent concern in the modern workplace. This mental drain can be particularly pronounced in roles heavily reliant on prolonged computer work or intense cognitive demands. In this context, encouraging physical exercise emerges as not just a remedy but a proactive solution.

One strategy involves advocating for physical activities among those engaged in computer-centric roles. Suggestions such as taking a revitalizing lunchtime stroll, swimming, engaging in a brisk jog or participating in a recreational sport post-work hours can significantly counteract the sedentary nature of these roles. Forward-thinking companies have started to integrate exercise facilities within the workplace, providing opportunities for employees to utilize stationary bikes or weight machines during their breaks. It's been observed that individuals adhering to a consistent exercise routine tend to exhibit a lower susceptibility to mental exhaustion and burnout.

By positioning physical activity as a potent tool to counter mental fatigue, workplaces are demonstrating a holistic approach to well-being—one that acknowledges the intricate interplay between physical and mental health. Incorporating and advocating such practices not only fosters a healthier and more resilient workforce but also underscores the paramount importance of holistic wellness in effectively combating the detrimental impacts of workplace stress.

> *'You cannot tailor-make the situations in life, but you can tailor-make the attitudes to fit those situations before they arise.'*
>
> —ZIG ZIGLAR

BURNOUT

Unlike the swift, abrupt burnout of a light bulb, human burnout doesn't occur with a sudden flicker in brightness followed by an immediate outage. Instead, it's a gradual, almost imperceptible process, akin to a slow dimming of light over time. While some instances may culminate in physical breakdowns such as heart attacks or ulcers, the majority of burnouts are primarily psychological in nature.

The signs of burnout are nuanced, weaving themselves into the fabric of daily life in subtle yet pervasive ways. Individuals undergoing burnout gradually lose their zest, vitality and drive, and these changes manifest in a myriad of ways within their professional sphere. They begin to harbour a disliking for their job, experience heightened friction with colleagues, nurture distrust toward team leaders and carry a pervasive sense of dread each morning as they contemplate the day ahead at work.

While excessive stress undoubtedly stands as a prominent trigger for burnout, it's not the solitary villain in this narrative. Frustration stemming from unfulfilled promises, overlooked expected promotions or salary increments, as well as the relentless pressure of making critical decisions that could lead to potential catastrophic outcomes—all these elements can significantly stoke the fires of burnout. Furthermore, extended work hours or being confined to unfulfilling roles serve as additional contributors to this complex equation. Yet, individuals equipped with a positive mindset often navigate these challenges more adeptly, albeit not immune to their effects.

Identifying the subtle signs of burnout might prove to be relatively more straightforward than finding an absolute cure. Its markers encompass a gradual diminishment in assertiveness, a growing tolerance for mediocrity, a noticeable waning of motivation to enhance performance, a decline in overall productivity and a gradual deterioration of relationships, both personal and professional. By actively implementing the aforementioned suggestions and strategies, individuals and organizations can proactively stem the descent into a state of stagnation and disillusionment, thereby fostering an environment that promotes well-being, resilience and sustained productivity.

TEST YOUR STRESS LEVEL

Engage in this stress assessment as a valuable tool to ascertain the proximity of serious stress-related issues affecting various facets of your life. Dedicate a moment to delve into these insightful queries, carefully assigning your responses in the designated box provided. Utilize the indicators 'SA' to denote Strongly Affirmative, 'A' for Affirmative, 'N' representing Negative, and 'SN' indicating Strongly Negative.

This self-assessment presents a comprehensive reflection of stress across multiple dimensions, serving as a pivotal instrument in identifying areas of concern and potential red flags that might signal the need for proactive intervention and stress management strategies. Embrace this opportunity to evaluate and introspect, facilitating a deeper understanding of the intricate interplay between stressors and your overall well-being.

1._____ Are you frequently fatigued throughout the day, lacking energy?
2._____ Do you find yourself less vocal or participative in business meetings compared to your previous engagement level?
3._____ Are instances of forgetfulness becoming more prevalent in your daily life?
4._____ Despite adequate sleep, do you still feel persistently tired?
5._____ Does your mental acuity seem consistently diminished or less sharp?
6._____ Do you often feel further behind in your tasks at the end of the day compared to the outset?
7._____ Have you noticed a decreased level of patience in your interactions with others lately?
8._____ Are you allocating less time toward hobbies or activities you once found enjoyable?
9._____ Do accomplishments or achievements rarely bring you satisfaction or pleasure?
10._____ Is your performance rarely operating at maximum capacity during your waking hours?

Allocate yourself ten points for a Strongly Affirmative (SA) response, assign seven points for an Affirmative (A) answer, attribute three points for a Negative (N) reply, and mark zero points for a Strongly Negative (SN) response within this evaluation framework.

Upon calculating your cumulative score, consider the ensuing ranges as crucial indicators: a score spanning from 0 to 15 signifies a state of either complete inactivity or a meticulously organized life; a range between 16 to 50 implies a lower likelihood of experiencing burnout, indicating a relatively stable equilibrium; a score spanning 51 to 80 suggests a precarious position where burnout could be looming on the horizon, warranting proactive measures to restore balance and prevent further escalation; finally, a score of 86 to 100 signifies an elevated risk, indicating a critical juncture where you might be teetering on the brink, akin to a walking stress bomb.

This comprehensive assessment functions as a powerful diagnostic tool, offering insight into the potential emergence of stress-related concerns in various spheres of your life. Embrace the findings as an opportunity for self-reflection and proactive intervention, enabling the recognition and potential mitigation of burgeoning stressors that might be impacting your overall well-being.

MANAGING STRESS

Effectively managing job-related stress necessitates the proactive implementation of measures aimed at mitigating its profound impact on one's well-being and overall productivity. While some medical professionals might prescribe tranquilizers or other pharmaceutical interventions, empowering oneself to self-manage stress through holistic practices holds significant promise.

1. **Prioritizing your well-being** stands as a foundational pillar

in stress management. Dedicate attention to maintaining a nourishing diet and commit to a consistent exercise regimen, ensuring your physical health remains at its peak, thereby fortifying your resilience against stressors.

2. Embracing an array of **relaxation techniques** can prove invaluable. Engaging in structured relaxation exercises and carving out dedicated time for solitude enables you to unwind and recharge, fostering mental rejuvenation amidst life's demands.

3. **Fostering self-respect and nurturing high self-esteem** serves as a robust defense mechanism against external pressures. Individuals fortified with a strong sense of self-worth often exhibit heightened resilience in the face of challenging circumstances.

4. Acknowledging the inevitability of **not being able to please everyone** underscores the significance of setting realistic boundaries. Establishing and maintaining these boundaries is pivotal in safeguarding your mental and emotional well-being.

5. Cultivating a **thirst for continuous learning** is a potent tool. Embracing ongoing educational experiences keeps the mind agile, adaptable and consistently invigorated, reducing the impact of stress-induced challenges.

6. Establishing and nourishing a **reliable support network** comprising friends and family can provide invaluable assistance during challenging periods, offering emotional succor and guidance.

7. Thoughtfully **assessing and accepting commitments** that genuinely align with your priorities is essential. Politely declining tasks that might excessively drain your time and energy is a proactive step toward stress management.

8. **Fostering creativity** in approaching tasks is transformative. Innovating and reimagining how routine responsibilities are handled allows for the development of fresh, creative methods to tackle new challenges, thereby mitigating their stress-inducing impact.
9. Embracing **change as an avenue for new opportunities** rather than perceiving it as a threat can reshape one's perspective, enabling a more adaptive and less stress-laden response to evolving situations.
10. Harnessing the **power of positive thinking** stands as a formidable antidote to stress. Replacing negative thought patterns with positive mental images capitalizes on the proven benefits of an optimistic mindset.
11. **Reassessing leisure activities** that inadvertently contribute to tension is crucial. If certain hobbies or leisure pursuits, such as competitive sports or high-stakes games, exacerbate stress, exploring genuinely relaxing alternatives becomes pivotal for stress reduction.
12. Granting yourself the **permission to lead a balanced life** is paramount. Finding joy in activities with loved ones and relishing moments free from work-related thoughts without succumbing to guilt nurtures a healthier work-life balance, essential for stress management and overall well-being.

Not only do these strategies serve as effective shields against the onslaught of stress, but they also function as guiding principles in orchestrating a lifestyle that prioritizes self-care and resilience. Through their consistent application, you not only mitigate the immediate impacts of stress but also foster a foundation for long-term well-being and sustained productivity.

Moreover, these practices offer an invaluable toolkit for self-empowerment, enabling you to navigate the complexities of a demanding professional life while safeguarding your mental, emotional and physical health. They facilitate a profound shift in perspective, encouraging a proactive approach to stress management rather than merely reacting to its manifestations.

By integrating these strategies into your daily routine and embracing them as essential components of your lifestyle, you catalyze a transformative journey toward a more balanced, fulfilling, and resilient existence. This holistic approach not only ensures a more harmonious coexistence between your professional commitments and personal wellness but also lays the groundwork for a thriving, flourishing life that transcends the constraints of stress.

> *'Adopting the right attitude can convert a negative stress into a positive one.'*
>
> —HANS SELYE

COPING WITH BURNOUT

Recovery from burnout is a multifaceted journey that necessitates a candid and comprehensive examination of the fundamental issues often at the root of this state of emotional and physical exhaustion. These key factors represent pivotal aspects that, when left unaddressed, can significantly contribute to the onset or perpetuation of burnout:

1. **Diverging Objectives Creating Conflict**: burnout often stems from a divergence between personal aspirations and organizational goals, causing a palpable misalignment. This dissonance creates a perception of restricted avenues for

professional growth and alignment, leading to a profound sense of limitation.

2. **Tedious and Unstimulating Tasks**: the inundation of monotonous and uninspiring tasks, bereft of room for exploration or intellectual stimulation, fosters an environment dominated by repetitive duties. This perpetual cycle of routine work contributes significantly to a stagnant professional sphere.

3. **Limited Responsibility and Influence**: a dearth of new challenges or inadequate opportunities to assume greater responsibility can lead to a pervasive sense of stagnation and discontent. The absence of avenues for exerting influence or taking charge can compound dissatisfaction.

4. **Shifting Personal Priorities Impacting Career Focus**: life's dynamic nature often introduces unexpected shifts in personal priorities. Emerging familial needs or unforeseen health concerns can momentarily divert focus from career advancement to pressing personal obligations, disrupting professional trajectories.

5. **Unforeseen Educational or Technical Requirements**: the landscape of career progression is frequently affected by unforeseen educational or technical prerequisites. Without anticipatory measures and adequate time allocation for meeting these demands, high achievers risk derailing their professional journeys.

6. **Underappreciation despite Remarkable Efforts**: instances where unwavering dedication and the successful tackling of arduous tasks fail to translate into proportional recognition, praise, compensation or promotion can lead to a profound sense of undervaluation and disillusionment among professionals.

In navigating such challenging scenarios, adopting proactive measures emerges as a pivotal strategy to reclaim equilibrium and foster meaningful change:

1. **Thorough Documentation of Discrepancies**: a proactive approach involves meticulously documenting instances and experiences that vividly underscore the disparity between dedicated efforts exerted and the corresponding lack of acknowledgment or recognition. This comprehensive record serves as tangible evidence of the mismatch between input and acknowledgment, highlighting the need for rectification.
2. **Deliberate Self-Reflection and Goal Realignment**: engaging in profound introspection becomes imperative, prompting a deliberate reassessment of personal aspirations vis-à-vis professional objectives. This introspective journey enables the alignment of individual goals with career pursuits, ensuring a cohesive and purpose-driven trajectory.
3. **Initiating Constructive Dialogues with Stakeholders**: proactivity manifests in the initiative to convene discussions with pertinent stakeholders. By taking the lead in arranging a meeting to address concerns regarding the perceived deficiency in acknowledgment, individuals proactively seize control of the narrative. This proactive stance not only demonstrates agency but also presents an opportunity to catalyze personal and professional growth. Actively steering these conversations rather than passively awaiting external recognition empowers individuals to effectuate change and nurture a more conducive professional environment.

RELIEVING STRESS AT THE OFFICE

Alleviating stress within the office space is a profoundly individualized journey, as diverse approaches resonate uniquely with different individuals. What proves to be a panacea for stress relief for one might not necessarily yield the same efficacious results for another. Nonetheless, amidst this inherent diversity in coping mechanisms, there exist numerous strategies that, when incorporated, can notably contribute to fostering a more harmonious and balanced workday:

Embracing Personalized Timeout Strategies

Take, for instance, Charley, who, when grappling with the weight of undue pressure, proactively implements a strategy centred around brief respites. Sensing the overwhelming burden, he initiates a deliberate pause, stepping away from his desk, enveloping himself in his coat and purposefully exiting the office building. His chosen remedy involves a short but revitalizing ten-minute walk around the block or the adjacent parking lot. This intentional breather serves as a restorative interlude, revitalizing his energy and granting him a refreshed perspective upon his return.

Likewise, situated in the bustling downtown area, Esther crafts her stress-relieving sanctuary by temporarily leaving the confines of the office. Her chosen escape involves a serene and calming session of window shopping in the nearby mall. This intentional diversion serves as a soothing break from the work-induced tension, allowing her to return with a renewed sense of calm and focus.

On the other hand, confronted with constraints imposed by a boss disapproving of absences during work hours, Stan devises an alternative approach. Within the office's confines, he engineers a change of environment by engaging in necessary errands across different departments. This strategic manoeuvre effectively redirects his mental focus, providing a mental breather that helps alleviate the mounting tension without contravening workplace norms.

Each individual's unique approach underscores the need for tailored and adaptable strategies to combat stress in the workplace. Embracing the diversity of these approaches offers a multifaceted arsenal of coping mechanisms, ensuring a more comprehensive and inclusive approach toward achieving a balanced work environment.

Incorporating Subtle Exercise Techniques

While overt physical exercises like jumping jacks might not align with the ambiance of a shared office space, discreet yet effective methods such as controlled breathing can be seamlessly integrated. Employing techniques like inhaling deeply through the nose and exhaling slowly through the mouth for several repetitions bestows a profound calming effect, fostering relaxation that permeates the entire body, assuaging stress levels.

Tailored Exercise Solutions

Consider Ted, who capitalizes on the privilege of access to a well-equipped company gym. During moments of heightened stress, he strategically incorporates a brief session on a stationary bike. This proactive measure allows him to effectively alleviate tension without engaging in strenuous physical activity, thereby rejuvenating his mental state without breaking a sweat.

Strategic Task Rotation

Acknowledging the overwhelming pressure encircling a particular project, Heather tactically employs the strategy of task rotation. Sensing her diminishing focus amidst an imminent deadline, she astutely sets aside the pressing project momentarily. Redirecting her attention to a different task for a brief interval of thirty minutes, she returns to the primary project with a revitalized perspective, having cleared her mind for a renewed and more effective approach.

Embracing Social Support

For individuals like Peter, seeking solace in the company of a trusted friend serves as a powerful stress-relief mechanism. He consciously chooses to confide his stress and worries in a close companion, understanding that while an immediate solution might not emerge, verbalizing his thoughts to someone else provides a clarity of perspective. Additionally, the casual nature of conversation often proves to be a swift tension-reliever.

Individualized Solutions

In the quest for stress alleviation, myriad unconventional approaches can prove remarkably effective. Consider the story of an individual who, when overwhelmed with stress, retreats to the privacy of their car. Within the confines of this personal space, they meticulously seal the windows before releasing a visceral scream—a liberating act of emotional release that helps purge accumulated tension, offering a cathartic sense of relief.

Embarking On Personalized Stress-Relief Journeys

Consider Dierdre, who, fortunate enough to possess a private office space, discovers solace and rejuvenation through the tranquil practice of yoga. Dedication of a precious few minutes within the confines of her office allows her to untangle the knots of stress that tend to accumulate throughout the day. This deliberate practice serves as a sanctuary, nurturing both her physical and mental well-being amidst the demands of the workday.

The Sanctuary of Mental Escapism

Contrasting physical seclusion, Jim finds his haven in the recesses of his mind. His escape from workplace tension is facilitated by mental transportation to a serene stream nestled near his summer retreat. He immerses his senses in the vivid imagery of water cascading over smooth, sun-kissed rocks—an internal oasis of peace and tranquility meticulously crafted within the landscape of his thoughts.

Harnessing Mindfulness and Spiritual Connection

For others, the path to tranquility unfolds through the practices of meditation or devout prayer. By harnessing the power of mindfulness or establishing a deep spiritual connection, individuals can effectively alleviate the burdens of workplace stress. These practices enable a profound engagement with the present moment or a higher spiritual realm, offering a sanctuary amidst the chaos of professional obligations.

Diversity in Stress-Relief Approaches

Each of these distinctive approaches, whether unearthed through personal experimentation or embraced from existing practices, stands as a testament to the rich and diverse arsenal available for stress reduction within the workplace. These strategies signify the vast spectrum of methodologies individuals can explore to alleviate stress, highlighting the uniqueness of personal preferences and inclinations toward specific stress-relief practices.

The Importance of Personal Resonance

The crux lies in uncovering a stress-relief method that resonates deeply with individual needs—a practice that speaks directly to one's unique emotional, physical and psychological requirements. This pursuit involves identifying a personalized avenue that offers not just temporary respite but a sustainable means to navigate the pressures and demands inherent in professional life. Embracing and tailoring these approaches fosters a more holistic and fulfilling approach to managing workplace stress.

> *'Holding on the anger is like grasping a hot coal with the intent of throwing it at someone else—you are the one who gets burned.'*
>
> —BUDDHA

USING YOUR POSITIVE ATTITUDE TO HELP OTHERS

Your Crucial Role in Team Rejuvenation

The pivotal role you play in rejuvenating a burnt-out team member cannot be overstated. Your own positive attitude serves as a beacon of hope, illuminating the path toward their recovery through a series of transformative and supportive actions:

Unwavering Support as a Cornerstone

First and foremost, displaying unwavering support stands as a paramount pillar. Engaging in sincere and empathetic conversations creates an environment where concerns are not only welcomed but actively addressed. Facilitating necessary adjustments demonstrates a genuine interest in their well-being, fostering a safe space for open dialogue and support.

Exploring Potential Metamorphosis in Job Functions

Consider the potential for a metamorphosis in job functions as a means of invigorating their professional landscape. Altering tasks or facilitating a transition to a different team can inject freshness into their routine, offering novel challenges and avenues for rejuvenation. This strategic shift can reignite their passion and sense of purpose within the organizational framework.

Empowering through Skill Acquisition

Offering opportunities for skill acquisition presents a dual-edged solution. Redirecting focus towards learning not only broadens their skill set but also augments their value within the company. This empowerment fosters a sense of growth, accomplishment and renewed enthusiasm for their role and contributions.

Advocating for Professional Counselling

If these interventions fail to yield progress, the prudent step is to advocate for professional counseling. This proactive approach can provide specialized guidance and support, acknowledging the complexity of the situation and offering targeted assistance tailored to their individual needs. Professional guidance can offer coping strategies and tools to navigate challenges effectively.

Personal Transformation and Self-Reflection

Understanding behavioural inclinations represents merely the initial step. Recognizing these tendencies serves as a clarion call, prompting proactive measures to cultivate a shift in attitude. Delving into the insights provided in this comprehensive guide and applying its principles paves the way to fortify oneself against stress and burnout.

Embracing the Transformative Journey

Embracing this transformative journey involves a concerted effort to transmute negative thoughts into positive actions. This transformative process, albeit demanding, yields invaluable rewards. It promises a life enriched with newfound positivity, resilience and a renewed sense of purpose. By embracing these principles, you not only fortify yourself but also contribute significantly to the holistic well-being and rejuvenation of your team members.

*'To be calm when others are not shifts
the advantage to you in two ways:*

—It stabilizes your position.
—It encourages allies impressed by your self-control.'

7

UPGRADING CAPABILITIES

*'It is not because things are difficult that we do not
dare, it is because we do not dare that they are difficult.'*

—SENECA

The Dynamics of Capability and Performance

The profound dichotomy between capability and performance underlines a crucial aspect: mere aptitude alone does not ensure actual accomplishments. The pivotal bridge between possessing competence and realizing tangible achievements often resides within the realm of attitude—the mindset that dictates the application and utilization of our skills or ideas.

Competence as the Foundation

Competence, firmly rooted in the inherent ability to achieve, serves as the foundational bedrock upon which success can be built. However, this potentiality finds its true manifestation only when coupled with the right attitude and converted into action. It's the fusion of proficiency and proactive mindset that sets the stage for substantial accomplishments.

The Symbiotic Interplay

The interplay between competence and performance is inherently symbiotic. They complement each other when aligned toward the pursuit of goals. Yet, competence alone, devoid of concrete results, remains inert and falls short of realizing its transformative potential. Possessing the skillset or knowledge is merely the foundation; the true essence lies in channeling it through action, driven by a proactive and determined attitude.

Attitude as the Transformative Force

In this context, attitude emerges as the linchpin that transforms dormant competence into active performance. It's the driving force that propels individuals to harness their abilities effectively, surmounting obstacles and translating potential into tangible outcomes. The mindset, determination and resilience to persevere through challenges serve as the catalysts that convert raw competence into meaningful and measurable achievements.

The Role of Action and Determination

Action, fueled by a determined attitude, emerges as the catalyst for transformative change. It's the conduit through which competence is converted into tangible results. A proactive mindset, combined with resilience and a relentless pursuit of goals, not only leverages one's skills but also navigates complexities and adversities on the path toward success.

Understanding this intricate relationship between attitude, competence and action empowers individuals to not only possess the necessary skills but also harness them effectively, thereby unlocking their true potential and achieving remarkable milestones.

Embodying the Spirit of Innovation

Consider the paradigmatic innovators and pioneers whose impact surpassed mere knowledge or skill. They exemplified unwavering determination and tenacity, leveraging their capabilities to drive groundbreaking advancements. Their success wasn't solely rooted in expertise; it was fueled by a relentless attitude—a commitment to their goals despite encountering setbacks or failures along the way.

The Crucial Fusion of Competence and Attitude

The amalgamation of competence and attitude paves the path toward impactful performance. It's the dynamic interplay between capability, unwavering determination and efficient execution that delineates genuine success. Even the most competent individuals might falter in converting their potential into substantial achievements without the driving force of a proactive attitude.

The Transformative Power of Competence and Attitude

Competence's true value lies not just in its mere existence but in its active utilization—propelled and transformed by the right attitude. The relationship between competence and performance gains profundity when infused with determination and vigour necessary to materialize aspirations into reality.

Nurturing Competence and Growth

Competence, akin to a flourishing garden, thrives and expands through a complex interweaving of factors within an individual's mindset, environment and approach. The enhancement of competency isn't merely a linear trajectory; it's a multifaceted amalgamation of awareness, adaptability and a conducive ecosystem that fosters continuous improvement.

The Role of Clarity and Self-Awareness

Clarity emerges as a cornerstone in this developmental journey. Individuals who are cognizant of both external expectations and their own objectives establish a clear roadmap toward improvement. Understanding one's strengths and acknowledging limitations initiates a quest for growth, fostering a mindset inclined toward continuous learning and development.

Empowerment Through Resourcefulness

Moreover, understanding where to seek assistance or resources while being adept at functioning autonomously empowers individuals to navigate challenges independently. This self-sufficiency not only boosts confidence but also nurtures a culture of problem-solving and innovation, propelling both personal growth and organizational advancement.

By embracing the fusion of competence and attitude, individuals pave the way for their own growth, transforming potential into tangible achievements and contributing significantly to the realms of innovation and progress.

The Crucial Role of Self-Assessment

Self-assessment stands as a linchpin in personal progression, providing a valuable feedback loop for continual improvement. The ability to measure one's performance against personal benchmarks becomes instrumental in steering a trajectory toward growth. This introspective evaluation fuels an ongoing cycle of refinement, shaping and honing skills and strategies for enhanced efficacy.

The Nexus of Accomplishment and Reward

At the core of competence's evolution lies the vital connection between accomplishment and reward. A conducive environment, fostering a culture of meritocracy, serves as a driving force, motivating individuals to strive for excellence. When the correlation between achievement and reward is palpable, it ignites an inherent drive to excel, cultivating a culture where the most accomplished individuals receive due recognition and incentives.

The Supportive Ecosystem for Competence

Competence flourishes within an ecosystem that embraces key elements such as clarity, self-awareness, adaptability and the symbiotic relationship between accomplishment and reward. It's the fusion of intrinsic motivation with an enabling environment that fuels the growth trajectory of competency, transforming it from a static attribute into a dynamic, ever-evolving facet within an individual's skill set.

The Cycle of Refinement and Growth

The perpetuity of competence's evolution lies within a cycle of self-assessment and adaptation. This ongoing process of introspection and refinement serves as a catalyst for personal and professional growth. Embracing an environment that values meritocracy and rewards achievement nurtures a culture where individuals are driven to constantly improve and contribute meaningfully to their endeavours.

Empowering Competence through Recognition

Recognition of accomplishments within this ecosystem not only reinforces individuals' confidence but also encourages a spirit of innovation and dedication. Acknowledging achievements creates a positive feedback loop, motivating individuals to continually push boundaries and excel, thereby enriching the collective landscape with their evolved skill set.

In essence, the dynamic evolution of competence thrives within a nurturing ecosystem that champions self-assessment, merit-based recognition and a culture that values growth and achievement. It's the amalgamation of these elements that propels individuals toward continuous improvement, transforming their competency into a dynamic force driving personal and collective success.

FOSTER EMPLOYEE COMMITMENT

Cultivating Alignment and Dedication

Fostering commitment within employees goes beyond surface-level proficiency; it's about nurturing a deep alignment between their personal motivations and the overarching vision of the organization. This alignment hinges on creating an environment that not only acknowledges competence but also ignites a profound dedication toward achieving shared organizational goals.

Foundations of Commitment: Transparency and Communication

To instill commitment, transparency and effective communication serve as foundational pillars. Employees require a clear understanding of the organization's mission, core values and objectives. When the larger organizational picture is vividly painted, it acts as a guiding light, instilling a sense of purpose and fostering a strong sense of belonging among the workforce.

Empowerment as a Catalyst for Commitment

Empowerment emerges as an instrumental factor in nurturing commitment. Granting autonomy and providing avenues for active contribution empower employees to take ownership of their roles. When their voices are valued, and they have a platform to express their ideas and opinions, a profound sense of agency emerges. This empowerment fosters commitment deeply rooted in a genuine investment in the organization's success.

Cornerstones: Recognition and Appreciation

Another cornerstone in cultivating commitment is recognition and appreciation. Acknowledging and rewarding contributions, regardless of scale, validates employees' efforts. This affirmation not only boosts morale but also reinforces the link between commitment and the recognition of dedicated efforts. It serves as a powerful motivator, encouraging continued commitment and dedication to organizational objectives.

Sustaining Commitment: Continuous Nurturing

Sustaining commitment requires ongoing effort. Regular communication, consistent acknowledgment of achievements and the continuous provision of opportunities for growth and development ensure that the flame of dedication remains alight within the organizational culture. This ongoing nurturing reinforces the commitment loop, fostering a culture where dedication is not just valued but actively cultivated.

Nurturing Growth and Development

Creating a nurturing environment that encourages continual growth and development is pivotal. Investing in employees' professional advancement through comprehensive training, mentorship programs and providing opportunities for career progression conveys a vested interest in their long-term success. This investment not only fosters individual growth but also reciprocates with heightened commitment, establishing a symbiotic relationship between personal development and the organization's overall prosperity.

Inclusivity and Belonging as Pillars of Commitment

Fostering a culture of inclusivity and belonging within the workplace significantly enhances commitment. When employees feel valued and respected, regardless of their role or position, it cultivates a profound sense of camaraderie and loyalty. This sense of cohesion transcends individual roles, translating into a collective commitment toward the organization's triumphs and endeavours.

Leadership's Role in Setting Examples

Leadership plays a pivotal role in fostering commitment by setting a compelling example. Leaders who embody dedication, integrity and a deep passion for the organizational mission inspire employees to emulate their commitment. When leadership practices what they preach and exemplifies the values they espouse, it establishes a powerful precedent, reinforcing the crucial link between commitment and the organization's success.

The Comprehensive Approach to Fostering Commitment

In essence, fostering commitment in employees transcends beyond the realms of mere competency. It's about nurturing an environment that not only harnesses individual skills but also cultivates a shared sense of purpose, autonomy, growth opportunities, recognition, inclusivity and exemplary leadership. Each of these facets forms integral components in forging an unshakable dedication to the collective success of the organization.

By incorporating these multifaceted elements into the organizational ethos, leaders can cultivate a robust culture that not only encourages commitment but also empowers employees to flourish, contributing their best towards the overarching goals and aspirations of the organization.

Embedding these established practices within organizational frameworks can significantly bolster workplace dynamics and foster a culture of productivity, innovation and cohesion. Let's expand on these points:

1. **Encouraging Minority Opinions** Actively seeking diverse perspectives during decision-making processes fosters a culture of inclusivity. Embracing dissenting views encourages a comprehensive exploration of ideas, preventing groupthink and nurturing a culture that values diverse viewpoints. This practice serves as a catalyst for constructive dialogue, paving the way for innovative solutions and informed decision-making.
2. **Rewarding Innovation and Creativity** Celebrating and publicly acknowledging novel ideas and successful innovations is crucial. Championing a culture where creativity is esteemed incentivizes employees to think outside the box, fostering an environment conducive to innovative problem-solving. This recognition inspires individuals to contribute their unique perspectives and fuels a culture of continuous improvement.
3. **Support for Personal Challenges** Demonstrating empathy by accommodating personal challenges within reasonable bounds showcases understanding and consideration. Flexibility in managing personal schedules contributes to an environment that values employees' well-being, fostering a sense of support and empathy within the workplace.
4. **Advance Notice for Schedule Changes** Communicating changes or overtime requirements well in advance respects employees' time commitments outside of work. Providing advance notice allows individuals to effectively manage their personal responsibilities, contributing to a balanced work-life equilibrium and reducing stress levels.

5. **Promoting Cooperation over Competition** Fostering a collaborative ethos by rewarding teamwork and cooperative problem-solving is paramount. Discouraging an overly competitive environment encourages collective goals, emphasizing the success achieved through collaborative efforts. This approach cultivates a sense of unity and shared purpose among team members.
6. **Identifying Key Individuals** Recognizing and supporting high-performing individuals vital to organizational success is crucial. Understanding their aspirations, providing growth opportunities and offering necessary support fortifies their commitment to the organization, fostering loyalty and dedication.
7. **Exemplifying Organizational Commitment** Leading by example in upholding a steadfast commitment to the organization's goals and values sets the tone for the entire workforce. Leadership actions serve as a model, shaping the organizational culture and reinforcing principles of dedication and allegiance.

By integrating these practices into organizational frameworks, companies create an environment that encourages diverse thinking, values creativity, supports individual needs and fosters a collaborative culture. These efforts not only enhance productivity but also contribute to a harmonious and engaged workforce, driving organizational success and sustainability.

> *'Human beings can alter their lives by altering their attitudes of mind.'*
>
> —WILLIAM JAMES

HOW TO DISAGREE WITHOUT BEING DISAGREEABLE

Let's elaborate on leveraging disagreement for collaboration and steps to navigate disagreements constructively:

Leveraging Disagreement for Collaboration

Utilizing disagreement to drive collaboration is pivotal in fostering a healthy work environment. Encouraging individuals to engage in healthy debates or constructive disagreements redirects their energies toward seeking common ground and consensus. This process not only enhances understanding but also encourages arriving at more comprehensive insights into complex issues, facilitating well-informed decisions and innovative solutions through collective effort.

The Attitude Shift: Embracing Disagreement for Growth

Transforming controversy into positive outcomes depends on the attitude and approach employed. Embracing disagreement as an opportunity for growth and learning reframes it from an obstacle to a catalyst for progress. It's within the space of open dialogue and respect for diverse viewpoints that organizations and individuals can harness the power of disagreement to drive positive change and achieve optimal results.

Navigating Disagreements Constructively: Steps to Follow

1. **Question Your Initial Impression:** acknowledge and pause to reassess your initial reactions in disagreeable situations. Taking a moment before reacting helps in representing your best self.
2. **Maintain Emotional Control:** strive for rationality

over emotionality when addressing personal problems or unsatisfactory performance. Keeping a level head aids in objective assessment and issue resolution.
3. **Prioritize Listening:** allow uninterrupted expression from the other person. Listening attentively fosters understanding without immediate resistance or debate.
4. **Seek Common Ground:** emphasize areas of agreement after hearing out opposing viewpoints. Finding commonalities establishes a basis for constructive dialogue.
5. **Embrace Honesty and Accountability:** identify and acknowledge potential errors or mistakes. Demonstrating honesty disarms opponents and fosters a conducive environment for resolution.
6. **Commit to Investigating Ideas:** promise a thorough examination of concerns and genuinely follow through. This shows respect for their perspective and acknowledges potential merit in their suggestions.
7. **Consider Delaying Immediate Action:** propose postponing action to allow time for contemplation and analysis. Scheduling a follow-up meeting enables comprehensive consideration of issues raised.
8. **Prepare for Further Discussion:** compile and note down challenging questions or concerns before subsequent meetings. This preparation ensures readiness to address specific points, fostering more productive discussions.

By following these steps, individuals can navigate disagreements by fostering constructive dialogue, empathy and an open-minded approach. This method promotes an environment conducive to conflict resolution, mutual understanding and respect, ultimately contributing to a more collaborative and harmonious workplace.

Engaging in contemplation during times of controversy can indeed be a powerful tool for introspection and constructive resolution. Here's an expanded exploration of self-analysing tools:

1. **Seeking Truth and Understanding** Consider exploring the possibility that the opposing viewpoint might hold some validity or truth. Evaluating the potential merit in their argument or perspective opens doors to a broader understanding of the situation, enriching your perspective.
2. **Assessing the Nature of Reaction** Reflect on the motive driving your reaction. Evaluate whether your response aims to address the problem or simply ease your frustration. Consider how your reaction might contribute to bridging the divide or widen the gap in understanding.
3. **Considering Personal Perception** Ponder the impact of your response on others' perceptions of you. Contemplate whether your reaction elevates their estimation of your character and professionalism or has the potential to tarnish it. Think about the long-term implications on relationships and reputation.
4. **Weighing the Outcome** Contemplate the potential outcome of the situation. Assess whether winning the argument or conflict is worth the potential price you might have to pay. Analyse the short-term victory against potential long-term consequences or fallout.
5. **Silence as a Strategy** Evaluate the effectiveness of remaining quiet during disagreement. Consider whether the disagreement might naturally dissipate over time and if your involvement might exacerbate or de-escalate the situation.
6. **Identifying Opportunities in Difficulty** Reevaluate the

challenging situation as an opportunity for personal growth or learning. Explore the lessons or insights you've gleaned from the controversy, viewing it as a potential catalyst for self-improvement.

By engaging in this introspective process, individuals navigate controversy with mindfulness and strategic thinking. The act of self-inquiry through these questions encourages a nuanced approach to disagreements, fostering introspection, empathy and the potential for constructive resolution. This reflective approach not only aids in conflict resolution but also cultivates personal growth and maturity in handling contentious situations. It fosters an environment where disagreements can lead to growth and positive change, benefiting both individuals and the organization as a whole.

BOUNCE BACK AND WIN

'Adversity puts iron in your flesh.'

—SOMERSET MAUGHAM

Brett Favre's journey in professional sports stands as a testament to resilience and the profound lessons learned from adversity. His experience with addiction to painkillers showcased a pivotal moment that defined his career and exemplified the correlation between setbacks and ultimate triumph.

Favre's struggle with Vicodin addiction was rooted in the physical toll of relentless hits on the field, portraying the depth of challenges athletes often face. Despite acclaim and success, he grappled with a personal battle that not only threatened his career but also his well-being. The decision to seek rehabilitation, driven by familial and social pressures, marked a pivotal turning point—a courageous step toward healing and redemption.

His willingness to confront and overcome his addiction mirrored his unyielding determination on the field. Emerging from rehabilitation, Favre not only conquered his dependency but also embraced sobriety, showcasing his resilience and commitment to personal growth. This transformative period became a cornerstone in his life, shaping not just his career but also his character.

Favre's subsequent achievements, including three consecutive NFL Most Valuable Player awards and a record-breaking streak of 141 straight games played, underscored his unwavering resolve and indomitable spirit. His quote, 'I may get knocked down a lot… but I'll always get back up again,' epitomizes his perseverance in the face of adversity.

His story serves as a beacon of inspiration, highlighting the invaluable lessons drawn from setbacks. It underscores the significance of resilience, the strength derived from confronting challenges head-on and the profound growth that emerges from learning and rebounding from losses. Favre's journey encapsulates the essence of resilience and the transformative power of overcoming adversity, resonating beyond the realm of sports to inspire perseverance and fortitude in facing life's challenges.

Bill Mauldin's journey from a mischievous teenager to a revered cartoonist is a testament to resilience, talent and the power of artistic expression. His early exploits as a prankster and subsequent expulsion from high school mirrored his spirited and rebellious nature, traits that would later shape his distinct voice in the world of cartooning.

Driven by a passion for drawing, Mauldin's determination

to support his family led him to take a cartooning course at a tender age, showcasing his resourcefulness and initiative. He honed his craft by illustrating an array of mediums, from menus to political posters, fostering a diverse skill set and an adaptive approach to his art.

His time in the Army during World War II became a defining chapter in Mauldin's life. Through the creation of the Willie and Joe cartoons, he skilfully captured the raw and authentic experiences of soldiers, resonating deeply with his fellow servicemen. Despite facing resistance from higher-ups who sought to stifle his portrayal of the soldiers' realities, Mauldin's cartoons found resonance among the troops for their poignant accuracy.

Favre's narrative transcends the realm of professional sports, encapsulating a universal truth: enduring victory often arises from the resilience cultivated through adversity. His journey symbolizes the transformative power of perseverance, determination and the courage to rise stronger from setbacks, showcasing that true success encompasses not just accolades on the field but also the triumph of the human spirit.

Mauldin's story similarly echoes the theme of resilience. His journey exemplifies the unyielding spirit of an artist navigating challenges and obstacles, transforming his setbacks into stepping stones for creative expression. Mauldin's resilience in the face of resistance underscores the fortitude needed to stay true to his artistic vision, a testament to the enduring impact of resilience, determination and unwavering commitment.

Both Favre and Mauldin's journeys serve as testaments to the resilience needed to overcome challenges, emphasizing that setbacks can often serve as catalysts for personal growth and achievement. Their stories inspire and remind us that resilience, determination and the courage to persist in the face of adversity are pivotal in forging paths toward success and self-fulfilment.

Mauldin's significant impact was bolstered by the unwavering support of General Dwight Eisenhower, who recognized the essence of Mauldin's work, despite objections from General George Patton. This support emphasized the profound impact of his cartoons on encapsulating the soldiers' lives during wartime. Mauldin's portrayal of their struggles and camaraderie was a testament to the power of art in authentically reflecting the human experience, resonating deeply with both soldiers and civilians alike.

His accomplishments, which include two Pulitzer Prizes, solidify his legacy as a pioneering artist. His work transcended mere illustration, evolving into a poignant commentary on the intricate facets of the human condition. Mauldin's ability to offer profound insights into soldiers' lives earned him widespread respect and admiration, reaching far beyond the realm of cartooning.

The honour of being laid to rest in Arlington National Cemetery, accompanied by a twenty-one gun salute, stands as a testament to the enduring legacy of Mauldin's contributions. His life exemplifies the profound influence of art in capturing truth, fostering empathy and leaving an indelible mark on history. Mauldin's story serves as a testament to the transformative power of artistic expression and the lasting impact of conveying truth through creativity.

His legacy continues to inspire artists and individuals alike, underscoring the enduring significance of artistic expression in documenting history and reflecting the human experience. Mauldin's ability to merge artistic prowess with an acute understanding of the human condition reinforces the notion that art, when wielded with authenticity and conviction, possesses the potential to transcend time and resonate across generations.

TEST NEW SKILLS

The genesis of Trivial Pursuit through the collaboration of Chris Haney and Scott Abbot holds significant lessons, emphasizing the potential missed when dismissing an idea due to assumed market saturation. Their journey challenges the prevailing notion within the board game industry that it had peaked, discouraging potential innovators. Haney and Abbot defied these beliefs, channelling their determination into creating something unique, despite Trivial Pursuit's initial lukewarm reception.

Their perseverance amidst setbacks, including sluggish initial sales due to design and cost issues, highlighted their unwavering commitment to their vision. Rather than succumbing to discouragement, they tirelessly refined their game, seeking every possible opportunity for exposure.

Their strategic marketing initiatives, such as distributing Trivial Pursuit to media outlets and celebrities, showcased their tenacity. The endorsement from Johnny Carson on The Tonight Show became a turning point, propelling the game into the public eye and triggering an exponential surge in sales.

This narrative vividly illustrates that initial setbacks and underwhelming responses don't necessarily indicate a lack of market demand. Instead, they can serve as stepping stones toward success if met with resilience, strategic thinking and unwavering determination.

Trivial Pursuit's eventual success, marked by the sale of an astounding twenty million games in the United States alone by 1984, stands as a testament to the transformative power of persistence, innovative ideas, and effective marketing strategies. Haney and Abbot's narrative underscores the importance of believing in one's vision, persevering through challenges and employing unconventional methods to transform a seemingly niche idea into a colossal success. Their story echoes the potential of unexplored market niches and the rich rewards awaiting those who dare to challenge conventional wisdom and persist in pursuit of their dreams.

'The gap between mediocrity and excellence is the difference measured by two things—indifference and determination.'

DESERVE RESPECT

Emotional intelligence has emerged as a pivotal factor in leadership effectiveness, reshaping conventional notions of what constitutes impactful leadership. While technical expertise is undoubtedly crucial, numerous studies across diverse companies globally have revealed a ground-breaking truth: exceptional leadership surpasses mere technical prowess. Instead, it significantly hinges on qualities embedded within emotional intelligence, notably compassion.

The differentiation between exceptional leaders and their peers predominantly relies on attributes that go beyond technical acumen, accounting for a staggering 85 per cent of what sets them apart. Emotional intelligence stands out as the linchpin, playing a pivotal role in delineating exceptional leaders. It embodies a nuanced grasp of emotions, encompassing both personal and social aspects, thereby profoundly influencing leadership efficacy.

The concept of 'emotional intelligence' is a blend of

personal and social competence, forming the foundation of effective leadership. Personal competence involves facets like self-awareness, self-regulation and motivation—essential elements that equip leaders to adeptly navigate their own emotions and effectively manage stress, particularly in high-pressure situations.

Additionally, the social competence aspect of emotional intelligence encompasses traits such as empathy and adept social skills. These qualities empower leaders to navigate intricate interpersonal dynamics, foster unity within teams and cultivate trust and collaboration among their subordinates.

The recognition and integration of emotional intelligence into leadership paradigms signify a shift toward acknowledging the pivotal role of interpersonal skills and emotional awareness in driving successful leadership. It underscores the importance of a holistic approach to leadership that encompasses both technical prowess and emotional acuity, indicating a transformative understanding of effective leadership practices in contemporary organizational settings.

Emotional intelligence's profound impact on workplace dynamics extends beyond its significance. Leaders equipped with high emotional intelligence not only foster an environment conducive to innovation, engagement and productivity but also exhibit an unparalleled ability to empathize, comprehend and communicate effectively. These skills not only nurture a supportive workplace culture but also elevate employee satisfaction and retention rates.

The acknowledgment of emotional intelligence as the cornerstone of exceptional leadership underscores the necessity for organizations to prioritize the development of these qualities in their leaders. Investing in programs and initiatives geared towards cultivating emotional intelligence can yield substantial dividends. Such efforts pave the way for a generation of leaders who steer organizations towards success while prioritizing empathy, compassion and the establishment of holistic team dynamics.

The rise of emotional intelligence as the quintessential trait of outstanding leadership signals a paradigm shift. It champions a leadership ethos that centers not just on technical proficiency but also on the transformative potential of compassion, empathy and astute social acumen. This recalibration drives organizations toward resilience, adaptability and sustainable success in an increasingly complex and interconnected world.

Individuals possessing personal competence exhibit a profound self-awareness that transcends mere recognition of their emotions. This competence encompasses the ability to delve deep into their emotional landscape, discern the intricate nuances of their feelings and navigate them with finesse. Beyond introspection, this self-awareness fosters a comprehensive understanding of personal strengths and limitations, cultivating a profound awareness of their capabilities.

Furthermore, within personal competence, high emotional intelligence manifests in adept emotional management. Individuals excelling in this realm exude not only assertiveness but also balanced self-confidence. They demonstrate mastery in steering their emotions, maintaining composure and exercising control, even in the face of challenging circumstances. This ability contributes significantly to their effectiveness as leaders and their impact on organizational success.

Conversely, social competence, an integral facet of emotional intelligence, stands as a testament to an individual's profound sensitivity and acute attunement to the intricate emotional tapestries that define interpersonal interactions. This multifaceted skill transcends the mere act of observation; it embodies an empathic resonance with others, delving deep into their emotional nuances, unmet needs, and diverse perspectives. Such a nuanced skillset empowers individuals not only to decode the unspoken language of emotions but also to adeptly navigate the subtle, ever-evolving dynamics that underpin human interactions.

The truly socially competent individual is an epitome of empathy, wielding this profound quality as a catalyst to forge genuine connections with others. Through a meticulous acknowledgment and thorough understanding of the emotional landscapes of those around them, they pave the way for a rich tapestry of relationships marked by trust, respect, and an unwavering mutual understanding.

Furthermore, the profound insight into the transformative power of pride, when unchecked and morphed into arrogance, underscores the paramount significance of social competence. Astute individuals discern that an unrestrained ego has the potential to repel allies and followers, rendering even the most seasoned leaders ineffective. Hence, they champion humility and authenticity as guiding principles, recognizing that genuine leadership flourishes within the fertile ground of empathy and humility.

The symbiotic relationship between personal and social competence forms the very bedrock upon which high emotional intelligence is constructed. It represents a delicate equilibrium between self-awareness and an intricate comprehension of others' emotional realities. Leaders who embody these intrinsic traits create environments that transcend the ordinary, fostering authenticity, empathy and profound connections—forging a paradigm where individual triumphs intertwine with collaborative successes and enduring relationships that transcend the boundaries of both personal and professional domains.

The realm of successful leadership extends far beyond the realms of technical prowess; it hinges profoundly on a sophisticated understanding of human relationships and emotions. Effective leaders emerge as consummate relationship custodians, wielding their emotional intelligence as a potent tool to not just motivate but also to guide and inspire.

They seamlessly assume the role of influential motivators, cultivating environments wherein individuals are not just encouraged but empowered to realize their full potential. Their ability to uplift others springs from an innate capacity to weave intricate webs of meaningful relationships—a vast network cultivated not merely for personal gains but as a testament to their commitment to fostering collaboration, trust and mutual growth. Their prowess in teamwork and collaboration amplifies their leadership, serving as a catalyst to propel collective achievements to unprecedented heights.

Moreover, successful leaders are endowed with a remarkable ability to regulate their emotions, meticulously keeping destructive tendencies at bay. This mastery over emotional control intertwines seamlessly with their unwavering trustworthiness and unparalleled flexibility—traits that not only cement their credibility but also underscore their adaptability in navigating through the diverse, often turbulent terrains of leadership. Driven by an unwavering commitment to enhancing performance, their readiness to act decisively, especially in the face of adversity, stands as a testament to their resilience and unparalleled leadership acumen.

Their resilience shines brightly amid adversity, illuminating their path with unwavering optimism. Challenges aren't seen as mere barriers but rather as fertile ground for growth and innovation, fostering an environment where difficulties are embraced as catalysts for transformation. Their steadfast positivity serves as a guiding light, uniting and inspiring their teams through the storms of uncertainty and change.

At the core of their triumphs lies a robust framework of high emotional intelligence, shaping a leadership style characterized by an unwavering commitment to respect, genuine empathy and unwavering authenticity. Their adeptness in navigating the intricate labyrinth of human emotions, coupled with a visionary zeal for progress and a relentless readiness to adapt, positions them as dynamic leaders capable of not just instigating but spearheading transformative change.

The evolution from mere effectiveness in leadership to resounding success hinges fundamentally on the mastery of emotional intelligence—a journey that transcends mere technical prowess. It demands an intricate dance of managing relationships with finesse, deftly regulating one's own emotions and embracing adaptability as a foundational trait. This fusion forms the nucleus that propels leaders toward effectuating profound, sustainable change that resonates far beyond their immediate sphere of influence.

BE A COACH

> *'What I need is someone who will make me do what I am capable of doing.'*
>
> —RALPH WALDO EMERSON

The transformative impact of coaching and training in moulding attitudes and nurturing growth within teams is unparalleled in its scope and influence. Managers, in their pivotal roles, don't merely steer the present course but actively shape the trajectory of their teams' future.

Adopting a coaching mindset isn't just a shift; it's a tectonic transformation, positioning managers uniquely as architects of positive change and ongoing enhancement within their teams. It transcends the confines of conventional management, embodying a dynamic, fluid process dedicated to unleashing the latent potential within each team member, cultivating their abilities and fostering an environment steeped in perpetual development.

The crux of coaching lies in its capacity to seamlessly convert affirmative attitudes into palpable, observable on-the-job advancements. It embodies an iterative journey that commences with setting achievable milestones, progresses through diligent guidance and unwavering support and culminates in jubilant celebrations of accomplishments. Yet, it's not a destination but a continuous expedition, propelling the team toward new aspirations and benchmarks, perpetuating an unending cycle of growth and evolution.

Through coaching, managers empower their teams to transcend boundaries and access their dormant capabilities. By facilitating a continuous stream of feedback, encouragement and expert guidance, they cultivate an environment that not only fosters learning but also fuels innovation. This iterative process serves as the catalyst not just for individual advancement but also for fortifying team unity and enhancing overall performance.

Furthermore, the role of a manager as a coach extends beyond the dissemination of knowledge; it's about ingraining a growth mindset that permeates the very fabric of the team's ethos. It's about cultivating a culture deeply rooted in continual learning and improvement, where triumphs are celebrated, and setbacks are embraced as invaluable learning junctures.

In essence, managers who wholeheartedly embrace coaching and training initiatives sow the seeds for both individual and collective triumph. Their unwavering commitment to nurturing talent and fostering a culture that thrives on perpetual growth doesn't just elevate team performance—it forges a future where every team member flourishes, contributing their utmost to the collective triumph of the organization. This enduring commitment lays the groundwork for sustained success that resonates far beyond immediate accomplishments, shaping a legacy of continuous advancement and excellence.

The coaching domains outlined by Franklin C. Ashby and Arthur R. Pell in *Embracing Excellence* present an expansive roadmap, offering an intricate framework for cultivating an environment steeped in growth, collaboration and the embodiment of effective leadership principles within organizational settings.

1. Management Coaching stands as a foundational pillar, encompassing the essential elements of empowering leaders to delineate tasks clearly, instill accountability within their teams, extend unwavering guidance and support, foster consensus and provide invaluable mentoring alongside trust, recognition and rewards. This concerted effort creates an atmosphere primed for heightened productivity and continual growth, setting the stage for success.
2. Empathic Listening Coaching delves into the art of honing active listening skills, underscoring the significance of speaking less and listening attentively. It places emphasis on asking pertinent questions, exhibiting enthusiasm,

mastering appropriate body language and seamlessly balancing seriousness with humour, thereby fostering deeper connections and a profound understanding among team members.

3. Collaboration Coaching pivots on nurturing robust relationships within and beyond the workplace confines, maintaining a consistent approach in interactions, forging strategic alliances, cultivating an extensive network, nurturing a mindset geared toward mutual benefit and fostering interactions that breed cooperation and synergy, thereby elevating collective achievements.

4. Conflict Resolution Coaching orbits around the development of constructive methodologies for managing conflicts, offering lucid, non-aggressive feedback and demonstrating unwavering support and respect, thereby nurturing an environment where conflicts are not just addressed but are managed constructively to propel growth.

5. Positive Attitudes Coaching is instrumental in cultivating a workplace culture that thrives on diverse perspectives, exudes enthusiasm, fixates on solutions rather than dwelling on problems and presents opposing viewpoints with a focus on forging mutually beneficial outcomes—a cornerstone in nurturing a constructive and optimistic organizational ethos.

6. Self-Confidence Coaching entails encouraging individuals to embrace calculated risks without succumbing to the fear of failure, fostering resilience and cultivating assertiveness in decision-making processes, thereby contributing significantly to a more confident and proactive team dynamic.

7. Being Respectful Coaching underscores the paramount

importance of recognizing and honouring diverse contributions, nurturing genuine respect for varied perspectives without an air of condescension and establishing an environment where every voice is not just heard but valued and respected.
8. Strategic Leadership Coaching is an intricate exploration into fostering a broad, long-term perspective, encouraging the articulation and execution of strategic plans and promoting innovation and forward-thinking initiatives—a pivotal driver for organizational advancement.
9. Establishing Priorities Coaching equips leaders with the tools to effectively manage time, establish achievable benchmarks, communicate expectations clearly and ensure accountability without resorting to micromanagement—fostering an atmosphere characterized by clarity and operational efficiency.
10. Upward Communication Coaching zeroes in on maintaining effective channels of communication with upper management, aligning with their priorities, adeptly presenting concepts and spotlighting the accomplishments of the entire team—a fundamental linchpin in fostering organizational alignment and ultimate success.

In essence, coaching in these multifaceted arenas serves as a powerful catalyst, igniting the transformation of workplaces into holistic, growth-centric cultures. These coaching tenets, by fostering effective communication, collaboration and leadership skills, play an instrumental role in not just driving organizational success but also nurturing the continuous development and evolution of every individual within the organizational fold.

In the realm of managerial coaching, the role of a manager transcends the conventional bounds of mere supervision; it evolves into a multifaceted engagement that serves as a conduit for transformation within the team. Beyond the oversight of tasks, coaching embodies a dynamic and iterative process that continuously nurtures learning and fosters growth among team members.

At its core, one of the primary facets of managerial coaching involves an intricate assessment of how effectively employees assimilate newly acquired knowledge or skills. Managers play a pivotal role in ensuring that these acquired competencies seamlessly translate into tangible improvements in job performance. Through diligent guidance, demonstration of best practices and a keen eye on areas necessitating refinement, managers exhibit an unwavering commitment to fostering the professional development of their team members.

Moreover, the efficacy of coaching lies in its ability to empower managers to tailor their guidance to suit the unique needs and performance of each individual. This personalized approach enables them to pinpoint specific areas—be it attitudes, skills, knowledge gaps or inherent abilities—requiring enhancement. Such tailored interventions facilitate a nuanced evaluation, paving the way for targeted strategies aimed at bolstering employee performance and instilling a culture that continually strives for improvement.

Central to effective coaching is the cornerstone of accountability. Managers utilize this pivotal opportunity to delineate precise responsibilities for each team member, thereby cultivating a profound sense of ownership and unwavering commitment among individuals. By establishing unequivocal expectations and holding team members accountable for their roles, managers sow the seeds of purpose and drive, contributing significantly to the cultivation of a cohesive, goal-oriented team dynamic.

Nevertheless, it's essential to acknowledge the inherent imperfections in both coaches and those under their guidance. Perfection, an elusive ideal, takes a backseat to the pursuit of continuous growth and improvement. Embracing the notion that learning is an ongoing journey for both parties involved forms the cornerstone of effective coaching.

Above and beyond these facets, effective coaching embodies the subtle art of recognition. Managers, in their roles as coaches, profoundly grasp the importance of acknowledging and crediting achievements. By generously offering commendation where it's due, they sow the seeds of a culture steeped in appreciation and motivation—a workplace environment that not only celebrates successes but also serves as a breeding ground for further progress and accomplishments.

Managerial coaching stands as a testament to a manager's commitment that surpasses mere oversight—it embodies a profound dedication to nurturing individual growth and fostering a workplace culture steeped in values of accountability, recognition and a relentless pursuit of continuous improvement. This commitment stands as a testament to the manager's unwavering dedication to nurturing the potential and excellence of their team members.

At the heart of effective coaching lies the intricate balance between influence and authority. Successful coaches set themselves apart not by wielding dominance but by harnessing positive attitudes that serve as sources of inspiration and empowerment for their team members.

Savvy managers recognize that authority isn't solely

derived from a position of power; it's cultivated through the demonstration of expertise and seasoned experience. Their profound understanding of their team's roles and responsibilities not only commands respect but also garners a deeper level of consideration for their suggestions and recommendations.

When a manager displays a comprehensive grasp of an individual's job functions, it communicates a genuine investment in comprehending the intricacies of the team's work. This showcase of knowledge goes beyond mere impression; it acts as a catalyst, encouraging others to heed their guidance with closer attention. It inspires team members to perceive their suggestions not just as directives but as informed insights stemming from a thorough understanding of the work at hand.

Furthermore, the art of effective coaching transcends the confines of traditional authoritarian approaches. Instead, it hinges on the potency of positive attitudes and inspiration. Coaches who lead with positivity curate an environment where team members feel motivated, valued and empowered to bring forth their optimal selves in their roles.

By nurturing a positive atmosphere, these coaches cultivate a culture where individuals don't just welcome guidance but are also inspired to contribute their unique ideas and solutions. This approach instils a profound sense of ownership and commitment, prompting team members to willingly align their efforts with the team's objectives, thereby fostering a collaborative environment driven by shared goals and collective success.

The synergy between authority and positive influence epitomizes the cornerstone of effective coaching. It transcends the mere exertion of authority; it encapsulates the art of inspiring and positively influencing individuals, fostering an environment where mutual respect, trust and seamless collaboration not only thrive but serve as catalysts for continuous growth and success within the team. This approach isn't just about eliciting short-term compliance; it's about cultivating a culture characterized by active engagement and empowerment, a culture that serves as the bedrock for sustained success and perpetual evolution within the team dynamic.

Embarking on a coaching journey involves a strategic approach that ensures substantial and enduring results. Consider the following pivotal steps as essential guidelines in navigating this coaching odyssey:

1. Comprehensive Background Review: begin by delving into detailed background reports concerning the employee. Unearth vital evidence related to their:
   - Progress or any perceived areas of stagnation in their role.
   - Specific skill sets they possess, highlighting areas that might benefit from enhancement.
   - Potential or existing leadership capabilities that could be harnessed or further developed.
2. Identification of Current Job Responsibilities: establish a crystal-clear understanding of the primary job responsibilities currently entrusted to the employee. This foundational step lays the groundwork for crafting tailored coaching and development plans aligned with their roles and objectives.
3. Analysis of Achieved Results: conduct a thorough assessment of the outcomes and achievements derived from the employee's dedicated efforts. Scrutinize the effectiveness of their actions and contributions within their role, identifying notable successes and areas warranting improvement.

4. Evaluation of Training Quality and Application: scrutinize the quality and efficacy of the training programs the employee has undergone. Evaluate the seamless application of this training within their day-to-day responsibilities and performance metrics, discerning the extent to which this acquired knowledge has been effectively integrated into their role.

These essential steps serve as guideposts, steering the coaching process toward a more comprehensive and informed approach. By meticulously engaging in these phases, managers can harness a deeper understanding of their team members' backgrounds, capabilities and areas ripe for development, ultimately laying the groundwork for tailored coaching interventions that spur continuous growth and sustained success within the team.

Within the realm of coaching sessions, a strategic approach plays a pivotal role in steering the process towards meaningful outcomes:

- Communicate the Purpose: it's paramount to clearly articulate to the employee the primary objective of coaching—to facilitate their performance enhancement and provide unwavering support in their pursuit of achieving their utmost potential.
- Outline Coaching Steps and Schedule: providing a comprehensive overview of the coaching process is crucial. By elucidating the sequential steps and proposed schedule, expectations are aligned and a clear path forward is established, fostering a sense of direction and purpose.
- Foster Dialogue: an open and interactive environment is cultivated by encouraging questions and promptly

addressing the employee's queries. Creating this conversational space nurtures engagement and ensures that communication flows seamlessly.
- Define Expected Results: clarity regarding anticipated outcomes is key. By distinctly defining the desired objectives and milestones, mutual understanding is established, laying the groundwork for shared goals and a collective vision.

When addressing areas requiring improvement, strategic approaches are instrumental in driving progress:

1. Prioritize Focus Areas: by concentrating on one or two key improvement areas at a time, the depth and impact of exploration are amplified. This focused approach allows for a more profound and impactful examination of critical facets.
2. Encourage Self-Reflection: guiding conversations toward self-critique involves prompting introspective questions. Encouraging employees to reflect on their experiences through queries like, 'What new aspects did you encounter in this scenario?' or 'What alternative choices could have led to better outcomes, and why?' fosters a deeper understanding.
3. Emphasize Observational Learning: maintaining a receptive stance during discussions allows employees the space to express their thoughts freely. Active observation often yields valuable insights, enabling the recognition of nuances beyond verbal communication.

Moreover, effective coaching involves meticulous documentation and forward planning for future sessions:

- Record Insights and Plan for Future Sessions: documenting observations and key discussion points

for reference is crucial. Note specific areas to cover in subsequent sessions, incorporating insights from previous discussions and outlining objectives yet to be achieved.
- Preparation for Meetings: providing advance notice of upcoming sessions, along with a clear agenda and time allocation, ensures preparedness and focus for both coach and employee, maximizing the effectiveness of the sessions.

To maintain a trajectory of sustained progress and continual improvement, implementing ongoing engagement strategies is pivotal:

1. **Acknowledge and Encourage Progress:** recognizing and commending any strides made by the employee is essential, reinforcing positive efforts and celebrating achievements, thus fostering an environment where progress is acknowledged and valued.
2. **Define Problems Explicitly:** articulating and delineating encountered problems or challenges explicitly is crucial. This clarity helps steer away from ambiguity, enabling a more targeted approach toward solutions and problem-solving.
3. **Address Difficulties Directly:** avoiding the temptation to overlook or sidestep difficulties is imperative. Directly addressing these challenges fosters a proactive stance toward resolution, promoting a culture that embraces challenges as opportunities for growth.
4. **Provide Continuous Support:** offering consistent assistance and support underscores a commitment to the employee's ongoing growth and development. This unwavering support serves as a pillar for sustained improvement.
5. **Establish Written Improvement Goals:** solidifying

a commitment to improvement involves setting clear, documented goals. These goals serve as guiding beacons, navigating the path toward progress and serving as a tangible reminder of objectives to strive for.
6. **Identify Specific Training Needs:** pinpointing and addressing specific training requirements effectively enhances skills and capabilities. By addressing these needs, employees are equipped with the tools necessary for continual improvement.
7. **Maintain Transparency in Competitive Settings:** in environments where competition is prevalent, transparently communicating individual standings in relation to others fosters a clear understanding of performance benchmarks, nurturing a culture that values transparency and growth.

By implementing these meticulous and comprehensive coaching techniques, managers play a pivotal role in cultivating a culture deeply rooted in continuous improvement, self-reflection and sustained progress within their teams.

Effective coaching serves as a catalyst that significantly influences employee morale and performance, cultivating a sense of empowerment and engagement within the workplace. When employees receive personalized guidance and support from authoritative figures, they often exhibit higher levels of job satisfaction and motivation, recognizing the vested interest of their leaders in their success.

An illustrative case reported in Inc. Magazine sheds light on the profound impact of coaching on organizational success. Bob Metcalf's decision to found Three Com Corporation was coupled with the recognition of his managerial limitations. Acknowledging the critical need for expertise in certain managerial aspects, he astutely brought in Bill Kroust, a seasoned professional, to address challenges he encountered.

However, this strategic decision wasn't merely about filling a position; it was about cultivating a collaborative learning environment. Metcalf, shaped by an academic background fostering a penchant for winning arguments, sought to acquire Kroust's expertise in salesmanship. This partnership symbolized a mutual learning opportunity, with both individuals recognizing the inherent value in each other's expertise, establishing a foundation for collective growth and success.

Kroust's profound expertise in salesmanship served as a conduit for Metcalf's invaluable learning journey, effectively bridging the gap in his managerial skill set. This coaching dynamic went beyond a simple exchange of knowledge; it encapsulated a collaborative learning experience, showcasing the essence of coaching—where hierarchical roles dissolved, paving the way for mutual growth and shared learning.

The symbiotic coaching relationship between Kroust and Metcalf wasn't a one-way street of knowledge transfer; it epitomized a dynamic, reciprocal learning journey that enriched both individuals involved.

Drawing from his seasoned expertise, Kroust didn't solely focus on imparting managerial skills to Metcalf. Instead, he delved deeper, instilling the importance of meticulous planning, navigating emotional intricacies and navigating potentially challenging situations—a reservoir of skills pivotal for effective leadership.

However, this coaching dynamic wasn't unidirectional. Metcalf reciprocated by sharing his expertise with Kroust, offering insights into public speaking, steering clear of trivial pursuits, and emphasizing the pivotal virtues of principles and integrity. Metcalf's mentorship extended further, fostering an environment that encouraged calculated risks and embraced failures as integral parts of the learning journey. Moreover, he conveyed the profound lesson of embracing humour, teaching Kroust the invaluable skill of finding levity amidst challenging situations and laughing at oneself.

Their collaboration, although not devoid of disagreements, showcased their ability to collaborate and learn from each other's diverse perspectives. This symbiotic interaction not only strengthened their individual skill sets but also enhanced the overall resilience and capabilities of their company.

The essence of their coaching relationship transcended hierarchical boundaries, underscoring the transformative potential of coaching at all organizational levels. It highlighted the intrinsic benefits of seeking and providing coaching opportunities, emphasizing that growth and development are accessible to all within the organizational ecosystem.

This compelling example illuminates the pivotal role of coaching in fostering a culture ingrained with continuous learning, mutual respect and professional development. It stands as a testament to the power of collaborative coaching dynamics, fortifying individual competencies, strengthening organizational prowess and nurturing a culture that thrives on learning and collaboration.

Ultimately, this example underscores the transformative power of coaching partnerships within organizations. It serves as a beacon, illustrating how embracing coaching as a two-way learning process not only bridges skill gaps but also cultivates an environment steeped in mutual respect, collaboration and an unyielding pursuit of continuous improvement. In essence, it highlights how effective coaching propels individuals and organizations towards unprecedented success by leveraging diverse skill sets and tapping into each other's reservoirs of expertise.

8

OVERCOMING PROBLEMS TOGETHER

'Do what you can, with what you have, where you are.'

—THEODORE ROOSEVELT

WHEN THINGS GO WRONG

Navigating change and confronting errors necessitates a strategic and empathetic approach, a thoughtful stance that requires careful consideration and deliberate action. When adversity arises, it's crucial to approach it not merely as a challenge but as a transformative moment—a chance to evolve and refine our methods rather than succumb to blame or frustration. Taking a deliberate step back and meticulously evaluating the situation with an optimistic mindset not only sets the stage for problem-solving but also cultivates resilience in the face of uncertainty.

The crux lies in steering clear of impulsive reactions and embracing a composed, methodical assessment of the situation. This deliberate approach allows individuals to delve deeper into the root causes, gaining profound insights that can illuminate underlying issues and pave the way for effective solutions. Reacting emotionally, while human, often exacerbates challenges, leading to outcomes that might hinder progress rather than catalyze it.

Resorting to punitive measures in response to errors can inadvertently breed an atmosphere of fear, stifling growth and hindering individuals from taking ownership of their actions in the future. A more efficacious strategy involves fostering a culture of understanding and growth rather than instilling guilt. Embracing the role of a supportive mentor or facilitator enables guiding employees through an explorative journey, where identification of improvement areas is not about highlighting inadequacy but empowering individuals with knowledge and tools crucial for enhancement.

Assuming this supportive role allows leaders to cultivate a learning environment where individuals feel not just permitted but encouraged to acknowledge shortcomings and strive for improved performance. This approach transcends addressing immediate issues; it lays the foundation for continuous improvement, nurturing a culture where mistakes are embraced as opportunities for learning and personal growth. Such an environment not only addresses current challenges but also nurtures an ethos of continual advancement and resilience in the face of future uncertainties.

Navigating challenging situations, especially when grappling with subpar work or facing off against hostile personalities, demands a tactful and strategic approach. Rather than swiftly resorting to criticism, it's vital to delve into the intricate web of underlying reasons behind performance issues without pinpointing blame onto individuals. Collaborative endeavours often entail maneuvering through a diverse spectrum of personalities, underscoring the importance of conflict resolution and the cultivation of a conducive environment for productive collaboration.

To adeptly navigate these complex scenarios, one can consider employing an array of strategies that extend beyond immediate reactions:

1. Offering Genuine Compliments: recognizing and sincerely appreciating individuals, even those displaying hostility or struggling with performance, holds the power to significantly elevate their self-worth and cultivate a sense of value. Genuine compliments serve as a bridge for constructive engagement and can positively shape future interactions.
2. Avoiding Confrontations and Arguments: directly engaging in confrontations with individuals exhibiting hostility often intensifies their behaviour. Striving to uncover common ground, even in challenging circumstances, becomes pivotal. Seeking understanding and shared perspectives can serve as a de-escalating tactic, diffusing hostility and opening avenues for constructive dialogue.
3. Steering Clear of Humiliation or Shaming: reacting with humiliation or public shaming in response to subpar work or hostile behaviour only deepens resentment and fuels conflicts. Such approaches not only fail to address the root causes but also foster a hostile environment that obstructs conflict resolution and collaboration.

The overarching goal is to approach these situations with an empathetic lens, prioritizing resolution over the exacerbation of conflicts. By abstaining from immediate criticism, offering genuine appreciation, sidestepping direct confrontations and refraining from humiliating responses, leaders can foster an environment conducive to constructive conflict resolution and fruitful collaboration. These strategic maneuvers lay the groundwork for bridging gaps and nurturing relationships, even in the face of formidable interactions or performances falling short of expectations.

DEALING WITH CONFLICT

Conflict, in its multifaceted nature, isn't always a foreboding sign of negativity; rather, it stands as an intrinsic element within human interactions, often unveiling opportunities for profound growth and positive transformation. How we approach and interpret conflict holds substantial sway over its effects and eventual ramifications. Rather than perceiving conflict solely through a narrow scope of hostility or disarray, adopting a more comprehensive viewpoint can unveil its potential for yielding constructive outcomes and fostering beneficial change.

Delving deeper into this concept reveals an array of facets worth exploring:

1. Shift in Perception: rather than perceiving conflict as an inherently negative force or something to be avoided, there's immense value in reframing it as a catalyst for substantial growth. Approaching conflict with a mindset geared toward extracting valuable insights, fostering creativity and propelling innovation can transform it into a constructive force. This shift in perception allows individuals to embrace conflict as a stepping stone, guiding them toward progress rather than hindrance.
2. Understanding the Nature of Conflict: conflict isn't a monolithic entity solely characterized by hostility; its essence spans a diverse spectrum of opposition and discord. It manifests through a multitude of forms—diverging viewpoints, contrasting opinions or even competing ideas.

Recognizing this multifaceted nature permits a more nuanced approach in addressing and ultimately resolving conflict.
3. Potential for Constructive Outcomes: despite its unsettling nature, acknowledging the potential for positive outcomes inherent in conflict is pivotal. Effective management of conflict can pave the way for amplified collaboration, heightened problem-solving abilities and enriched relationships. Meaningful engagement in discussions arising from conflict nurtures mutual understanding and respect among involved parties.
4. Opportunities for Learning and Growth: embracing conflict as an avenue for learning and personal development reshapes it into a platform for self-reflection and advancement. It challenges individuals to reevaluate their perspectives, embrace alternative viewpoints and adapt their approaches. This process ultimately catalyzes personal and professional growth, amplifying one's capacity to navigate future conflicts more adeptly.

By adopting a perspective that not only acknowledges but actively embraces the potential for constructive outcomes nestled within conflict, individuals gain the ability to navigate these encounters with a profound sense of openness and unwavering optimism. This approach transcends merely reframing conflict; it metamorphoses it into an arena teeming with possibilities for catalyzing positive change. Furthermore, it has the transformative power to instil and nurture a culture that deeply values diverse perspectives, serves as a breeding ground for innovation, and champions the art of collaborative problem-solving.

When aiming for efficacy in conflict resolution, incorporating strategies to mitigate negative repercussions becomes a pivotal aspect of successful navigation. Here, we present reliable principles designed to serve as a steadfast compass in your conflict resolution endeavours:

1. **Face-to-Face Interaction for Clarity:** opting for in-person interactions during conflicts facilitates a deeper understanding of perspectives, fostering nuanced communication and enhancing clarity in dialogue.
2. **Express Views for Relationship Building:** the transparent sharing of viewpoints at the conflict's onset lays the groundwork for managing relationships, creating a platform for potential resolution rooted in mutual understanding.
3. **Balanced Discussion Platforms:** endeavour to minimize status disparities among conflicting parties during discussions, ensuring an equitable platform for dialogue and fair decision-making.
4. **Avoiding Blame Assignment:** acknowledging that assigning blame seldom contributes constructively to problem-solving, the focus remains on seeking solutions and forging ahead rather than dwelling on assigning fault.
5. **Address Conflicts Proactively:** tackling conflicts at their source whenever feasible helps prevent prolonged disputes and unnecessary escalation, resorting to managerial intervention only when essential.
6. **Maintain Flexibility in Solutions:** initially postponing commitment to specific solutions allows for flexibility, enabling exploration of diverse resolution options that may better suit the context.
7. **Establish Common Ground:** early identification and emphasis on areas of mutual agreement serve as a

cornerstone for cooperation within the conflict resolution process.

8. **Highlight Mutual Benefits:** emphasizing the mutual benefits of resolving conflicts underscores the reasons for collaboration, promoting a cooperative atmosphere over confrontational ones.
9. **Neutral and Impartial Language:** utilizing neutral and non-judgmental language in discussions prevents unintentional escalation of emotions, fostering a conducive environment for resolution.
10. **Specific Error Addressing:** when addressing errors contributing to conflicts, specificity trumps broad, sweeping statements to prevent further tensions from escalating.
11. **Leverage Past Successes:** building coalitions based on past successful conflict resolutions equips individuals to effectively manage future challenges, utilizing proven strategies for resolution.
12. **Self-Reflection for Objectivity:** prioritizing self-reflection helps identify personal biases or emotions that might hinder resolution efforts, ensuring a more objective approach to conflict resolution.

These principles stand as a comprehensive guide for effective conflict resolution, championing understanding, fairness and cooperation among conflicting parties. Embracing these strategies not only mitigates negative repercussions but also fosters an environment conducive to collaborative problem-solving and constructive conflict management.

GIVING CRITICISM

Enhancing receptivity to criticism stands as a crucial aspect of personal and professional growth, achievable through the thoughtful implementation of the following methods:

1. **Positive Conversation Initiation:** commencing conversations on a positive note, by seeking evaluations of accomplishments, nurtures an environment where individuals feel acknowledged and valued for their successes. This positive start sets the stage for constructive feedback, fostering an atmosphere conducive to growth.
2. **Discuss Unsuccessful Projects:** following discussions on achievements, delving into unsuccessful projects or errors becomes essential. Inquiring about the measures that could have potentially averted these mistakes encourages introspection and learning from past experiences, facilitating a culture of continuous improvement.
3. **Offer Recommendations and Suggestions:** contributing your own recommendations or alternative strategies showcases your commitment to improvement. This active engagement not only demonstrates your vested interest but also nurtures a collaborative environment that encourages collective problem-solving, fostering an open culture receptive to diverse viewpoints.
4. **Inquire About Training or Assistance:** displaying interest in the type of training or support needed signifies a readiness to invest in an individual's development. It acknowledges that improvement often requires resources and assistance, creating a receptive environment where feedback is perceived as an avenue for growth rather than criticism.

5. **Establish Specific Action Steps:** collaboratively outlining specific actions to improve outcomes showcases a dedication to change. Setting clear, defined steps not only enhances accountability but also provides a structured roadmap for progress, empowering individuals to take ownership of their development journey.

Incorporating these multifaceted methods into discussions surrounding performance evaluation or feedback sessions holds the potential to significantly augment receptivity to criticism. This holistic approach acknowledges achievements, addresses areas for improvement and cultivates a supportive environment conducive to continuous learning and growth. By reframing criticism as an opportunity for development and positive change, this approach transforms what might be perceived as a negative experience into a catalyst for personal and professional enhancement.

RESPONDING TO CRITICISM

Dale Carnegie's quote adeptly encapsulates a prevailing reaction to criticism—an often universal perception that tends to view it through a negative or discouraging lens. Yet, within the realms of conflict resolution and the art of handling criticism, lies not only the refinement of skill but the paramount significance of the attitude with which it is approached. Undoubtedly, criticism, when approached with the right mindset, possesses the potential to transcend its initial daunting appearance and become a profound source of immense benefit and unparalleled growth.

1. **Cultivating a Growth Mindset:** embracing criticism not as a setback but as an invaluable chance for growth lies at

the core. When individuals view feedback as a gateway to learning, adapting and ultimately improving, they cultivate a mindset focused on growth. Criticism transforms from an obstacle into a pivotal stepping stone for development.

2. **Learning from Different Perspectives:** criticism often acts as a beacon illuminating alternative viewpoints. Welcoming these diverse perspectives allows individuals to expand their understanding and glean insights they might not have considered otherwise. It presents an opportunity to view situations from varying angles, enriching their perspectives.

3. **Identifying Areas for Improvement:** constructive criticism serves as a guidepost, pinpointing areas ripe for enhancement. Rather than feeling disheartened, individuals can leverage these pointers to isolate specific aspects that warrant attention, thereby fortifying their skills or refining their approaches.

4. **Enhancing Self-Awareness:** thoughtfully receiving criticism prompts introspection. It encourages individuals to scrutinize their actions, reactions and behaviours, leading to heightened self-awareness and a more profound comprehension of their impact on others.

5. **Building Resilience and Adaptability:** navigating criticism with a positive outlook fosters resilience. It imparts the ability to confront challenges, adapt to diverse opinions and flourish in dynamic environments—a pivotal skill for both personal and professional growth.

6. **Fostering Improved Communication:** addressing criticism constructively paves the way for open communication. It creates an atmosphere where feedback flows freely, nurturing a space for more transparent and effective interactions among individuals or within teams.

By embracing criticism as an opportunity for growth rather than a setback, individuals harness its latent benefits. It evolves into a catalyst propelling personal and professional development, nurturing a culture that thrives on continual improvement, adaptability and resilience. Integrating this perspective on criticism not only aids in navigating conflicts but also cultivates a more positive and solution-oriented attitude towards challenges.

CONSIDER THE SOURCE

Evaluating criticism involves an intricate web of considerations that extend beyond the surface-level content of the critique. A deeper exploration into the source and context of criticism unveils layers of insights crucial in formulating a more comprehensive response:

1. **Understanding the Source's Credentials:** delving into the credentials and background of the critic provides a nuanced perspective on their knowledge and expertise within the subject matter. Recognizing their level of experience and access to updated information aids in gauging the credibility and relevance of the critique.
2. **Recognizing Patterns in Criticism:** a comparison of current criticism with past instances assists in identifying recurring patterns. Consistent feedback from the same or different sources unveils common themes, offering invaluable cues for improvement or validation of existing practices.
3. **Unveiling Motives Behind Criticism:** analysing the underlying motives behind the criticism holds pivotal significance. Understanding the stakeholders involved and

who stands to gain or lose from the feedback sheds light on potential biases or vested interests, facilitating a more balanced interpretation of the critique.
4. **Assessing Emotional Context:** distinguishing between reactionary outbursts and composed evaluations becomes essential. Criticism delivered in a calm, collected manner often carries more weight, indicating a well-thought-out perspective. In contrast, emotionally charged feedback may reflect immediate emotions rather than a meticulously considered assessment.
5. **Calibrating Responses to the Critique:** tailoring responses based on the nature and context of the criticism remains imperative. A well-reasoned, composed critique might warrant a similarly analytical response, while emotionally charged feedback might necessitate a more empathetic and understanding approach.
6. **Considering Diverse Perspectives:** acknowledging the existence of diverse perspectives fosters a broader understanding of the critique. It encourages individuals to embrace varying viewpoints, cultivating a culture of inclusivity and constructive dialogue, essential for comprehensive evaluation and growth.

Responding to criticism, particularly within leadership roles, holds profound implications for both personal and organizational growth. Here's a more comprehensive exploration of its impact:

- Navigating Vulnerability in Leadership: leaders often find themselves in a position of heightened vulnerability when subjected to criticism. Their decisions and actions are under constant scrutiny. Embracing this vulnerability

as an inherent aspect of leadership is crucial, recognizing that mistakes and feedback serve as integral components of the growth process.
- Reframing Criticism as an Opportunity: in leadership roles, criticism ought to be perceived as an avenue for improvement rather than a personal attack. Understanding that feedback, even when delivered harshly, harbours valuable insights for professional development bolsters a leader's capacity to navigate challenging situations with resilience.
- Significance of Recovery and Response: how leaders bounce back from accusations or criticism holds immense significance. Their response to criticism not only shapes the organizational culture but also sets a precedent for how mistakes are handled. A composed, constructive response lays the groundwork for a culture centred on learning and resilience.
- Learning from Adversity: adversity, encompassing criticism and accusations, presents an invaluable opportunity for learning. Leaders adept at managing such situations often emerge stronger and more resilient. It provides a chance for self-reflection, a reassessment of decisions, and the refinement of strategies for future endeavours.
- Evolving Through Constructive Feedback: embracing criticism, especially when it offers constructive feedback, becomes a catalyst for a leader's growth. It fosters introspection, prompts consideration of diverse perspectives and enables continuous improvement in leadership approaches.
- Setting a Tone for Organizational Culture: a leader's response to criticism lays the cornerstone for the

organizational culture. Embracing a growth-oriented mindset in the face of criticism cultivates an environment where feedback holds value, mistakes are regarded as learning opportunities, and resilience is not only encouraged but celebrated.

Reframing criticism as a fertile ground for growth is a pivotal strategy for leaders aiming to foster a culture of continuous improvement within their organizations. By embracing criticism as a catalyst for personal and collective development, leaders not only navigate their own vulnerabilities but also learn invaluable lessons from adversity, steering the organization towards an ethos that thrives on challenges as opportunities for advancement rather than as stumbling blocks.

Resilience, as the cornerstone of progress, becomes a defining factor in how leaders rebound from adversity. Success, after all, hinges not only on managing favourable tasks but also on tackling the challenging and often unpleasant duties that come their way. Striking a balance amid these varied challenges emerges as pivotal for sustained growth and progress.

Navigating through such challenges, particularly in the face of criticism or conflict, demands a deliberate and composed approach. When feeling off-balance, taking a momentary pause becomes instrumental. It provides the opportunity for a focused analysis of the core problem. Tackling issues systematically, without succumbing to tension or worry, optimizes energy and enhances productivity.

Criticism holds substantial potential for organizational improvement. Astute managers recognize the criticality of swift conflict resolution, promptly addressing disagreements to reaffirm their team's value while defusing conflicts. Embracing feedback as a universal tool for growth is foundational in cultivating a culture of perpetual enhancement.

However, the lingering of grudges often arises due to reluctance in making amends. Pride can inadvertently impede progress, leading to stalemates. Effective managers comprehend the significance of open conflict resolution, taking proactive steps to foster a culture where mistakes are forgiven, understanding that nurturing resentments only impedes collective growth.

Forgiveness and growth emerge as keystones in effective leadership. Cultivating an environment where mistakes are seen as valuable lessons becomes a hallmark of exemplary leadership. Encouraging open communication, forgiveness, and the ethos of learning from missteps becomes pivotal in creating a resilient and innovative team dynamic that propels the organization forward.

Swift conflict resolution stands as another hallmark of effective leadership. Leaders adept at promptly addressing conflicts not only mitigate potential disruptions but also reinforce the team's unity and effectiveness. Resolving conflicts swiftly fosters an atmosphere of trust and collaboration, fuelling productivity and innovation.

Equally significant is the cultivation of a forgiving culture within an organization. Leaders who foster an environment where forgiveness is valued acknowledge the human aspect of mistakes and create a space where individuals feel encouraged to learn from missteps. Such an ethos promotes resilience, innovation and a willingness to take calculated risks.

Collectively, these facets of effective leadership intertwine to optimize individual and team performance. They establish a framework that not only addresses immediate challenges but also propels the organization toward sustained growth by nurturing a culture of continuous improvement, innovation and adaptability in the face of change.

> *'Being defeated is often only a temporary condition.
> Giving up is what makes it permanent.'*
>
> —MARILYN VOS SAVANT

9

MOTIVATING OTHERS

*'First say to yourself what you would be;
and then do what you have to do.'*

—EPICETUS

THE INFLUENCE OF ATTITUDE IN LEADERSHIP DYNAMICS

As a manager or supervisor, your role transcends the mere execution of tasks; it encompasses the shaping of team culture and productivity through your demeanour, approach and interactions. Even prior to officially assuming a managerial position, your attitude and behaviour wield significant influence within your immediate circle, moulding perceptions regarding collaboration, leadership and collective goals. These attributes serve as foundational pillars, particularly during the transition into a managerial role, as your capacity to inspire and guide others profoundly impacts your success.

Ascending to a managerial position isn't solely about the acquisition of a title; it's about earning recognition as someone who ignites excellence in others. The effectiveness of your leadership often pivots on the perception of your empathy and authentic concern for your team's well-being. Employees tend to be more motivated when they sense understanding, value, and support, making these qualities pivotal in nurturing a positive and conducive work environment.

In the realm of supervision, your primary role orbits around fostering unity and a shared sense of purpose among team members to realize collective objectives. This journey commences by forging meaningful connections with your colleagues. Grasping their individual strengths, weaknesses, aspirations and even understanding personal challenges like family dynamics or external concerns lays the foundation for cultivating a motivated, engaged and cohesive team.

By dedicating time and effort to comprehend your team members on a personal level, you not only cultivate rapport but also demonstrate a genuine interest in their success and well-being. This approach lays the groundwork for fostering a team that not only collaborates but also actively supports each other's growth, collectively striving towards overarching goals. Your role as a supervisor extends beyond mere task delegation; it involves creating an environment where every individual feels empowered and motivated to contribute their utmost, ultimately nurturing a more harmonious and productive workplace.

Developing a cohesive team transcends the mere sharpening of job-related skills; it encompasses a deep dive into the intricacies of personal aspirations, family dynamics and individual concerns that extend beyond professional duties. Understanding and acknowledging these facets of your team members' lives signify a level of empathy and consideration that forms the bedrock of a strong and supportive team dynamic.

One pivotal aspect of fostering this positive environment involves the consistent recognition of exceptional work and the continual display of respect towards team members. Timely acknowledgment and celebration of commendable achievements not only elevate morale but also reinforce a profound sense of trust and validation within the team. Moreover, demonstrating unwavering respect towards each team member, irrespective of their role or seniority, plays a pivotal role in cultivating a positive work culture. This culture of mutual respect creates an environment where every individual feels valued, contributing to a sense of camaraderie and unity among team members.

Additionally, providing support during challenging times stands as a cornerstone in solidifying the perception of your unwavering commitment to your team's success. Extending support during moments of difficulty or obstacles not only showcases your dedication but also reinforces the trust your team places in your leadership. This support during adversity becomes instrumental in strengthening the bond between you and your team, instilling a sense of security and assurance that they have a reliable support system in challenging situations.

In essence, by acknowledging accomplishments, consistently demonstrating respect and offering unwavering support during trying times, you not only bolster the morale and confidence of your team but also cultivate an environment where individuals feel valued, supported and motivated to contribute their best efforts. This approach lays the groundwork for nurturing a cohesive and resilient team capable of overcoming obstacles and achieving collective success.

NAVIGATING THE FIELD OF OVERACHIEVERS

High achievers serve as the backbone of any organization, representing not just outstanding performance but also embodying the potential for future growth and innovation. However, it's a prevalent misconception that managing high achievers necessitates less attention or management focus compared to those with lower performance. In reality, these individuals, while exceptionally skilled and productive, require strategic handling and tailored support to sustain their momentum and foster their continued growth within the organization.

Overlooking the needs of high achievers can lead to missed opportunities and potential challenges for both the individual and the organization. Here's why: these high performers, propelled by an insatiable thirst for improvement and challenge, actively seek environments that facilitate their ongoing development. When these individuals sense stagnation or lack of support, they might become disengaged or seek opportunities elsewhere. Their ambition and drive might result in dissatisfaction if they perceive that their potential isn't being fully realized or acknowledged within their current role.

Moreover, high achievers often operate at the forefront of innovation and progress within an organization. Neglecting their needs or failing to provide adequate challenges might inadvertently lead to underutilizing their exceptional talents. Effectively harnessing their abilities entails offering space for innovation, presenting challenges that align with their aspirations and ensuring continuous refinement of their skills.

Additionally, these high performers, despite their exceptional performance, might benefit from unique management strategies. Tailored goals, specialized training or opportunities that empower them to lead and contribute meaningfully can significantly enhance their performance. Failure to provide them with the necessary attention or avenues for growth might result in frustration or diminished motivation, ultimately impeding their overall productivity and potential contributions to the organization.

Recognizing and strategically managing high achievers is as vital as supporting and nurturing lower performers within an organization's dynamics. These high performers are not just contributors; they serve as the driving force behind innovation, growth, and leadership. Hence, comprehending their unique needs, fostering avenues for their growth and duly recognizing their invaluable contributions are crucial steps that ensure their sustained success while propelling the organization forward.

1. **Progressive Assignments and Oversight:**
   - assigning high achievers with challenging yet manageable tasks allows them to stretch their capabilities while offering guidance and oversight. This balance grants them the autonomy to innovate and excel.
   - Offering projects aligned with their career aspirations serves as stepping stones for their professional advancement within the organization.
2. **Recognition and Feedback:**
   - Publicly acknowledging and rewarding outstanding performance reinforces a culture of achievement. Highlighting their contributions in team meetings or through internal communications showcases their impact.
   - Providing feedback or critique in private settings preserves their dignity and focuses on constructive improvement rather than public scrutiny.
3. **Temporary Promotions and Growth Opportunities:**
   - Offering temporary promotions or lateral moves assesses

high achievers' capabilities in leadership or higher-level roles, identifying potential future leaders within the organization.
- Evaluating their response to novel challenges and increased responsibilities helps gauge their leadership potential.

4. **Fostering a Culture of Innovation:**
   - Encouraging high achievers to share innovative ideas and solutions harnesses their genuine passion for excellence, fostering an environment where their contributions are valued.
   - Cultivating an environment where overachievers feel heard and appreciated leverages their insights and innovations to drive progress, inspiring others to strive for excellence.

5. **Continuous Skill Development:**
   - Facilitating continuous skill enhancement through workshops, training programs or mentorship initiatives aligns with their interests and the organization's needs.
   - Supporting their pursuit of new skills fosters a culture of lifelong learning that aligns with their career aspirations.

In essence, strategic empowerment and recognition of high achievers are pivotal in unlocking their potential. By providing challenging opportunities, acknowledging their contributions, assessing their leadership capabilities and nurturing a culture of innovation, organizations stand to reap immense benefits from the talents and drive of their top performers, thereby fostering a dynamic and progressive work environment.

IMPROVING EFFECTIVE COMMUNICATION

Effective communication embodies more than just the verbal exchange of words; it encapsulates a fusion of attitude, technique and intent that serves as the bedrock for successful interactions. It's about cultivating an environment where conversations are purpose-driven, transcending simple exchanges to become rich and meaningful engagements. Central to this lies the pivotal aspect of acknowledging and addressing the queries and concerns raised by others.

The essence of purpose-driven interaction revolves around considering the perspectives and needs of all participants. By prioritizing the concerns, queries and viewpoints of each individual, conversations evolve into inclusive dialogues. This inclusive approach nurtures an environment where every voice holds value, fostering a sense of engagement and collaboration among team members.

Furthermore, effective communication is deeply rooted in a commitment to understanding and empathy. It transcends the mere transmission of information; it involves grasping the underlying motives and emotions behind the spoken words. By fostering an atmosphere where individuals feel heard, understood and respected, conversations transform into productive exchanges that elevate team dynamics and problem-solving capabilities.

At its core, effective communication is intertwined with attitude—an attitude marked by openness, empathy and receptivity toward others' perspectives. It involves employing techniques that extend beyond verbal expression, encompassing active listening, mindful body language and adaptability in approach. When purpose-driven dialogue becomes the norm, it fosters a collaborative environment where ideas flourish, conflicts find resolution and collective goals are achieved. This collective effort fuels an environment where communication becomes a catalyst for success, propelling the organization towards its objectives.

To enhance collaboration among colleagues, implementing several strategic approaches can significantly bolster team dynamics and overall productivity. Here are some strategies to consider:

1. **Timely Dissemination and Accessibility:**
   - Timely sharing of crucial information enables proactive decision-making and better preparedness among colleagues, fostering a proactive work environment.
   - Ensure accessibility through efficient communication channels or platforms, facilitating easy access to essential knowledge and updates to streamline workflow processes.
2. **Audience-Centric Approach:**
   - Tailoring conversations to resonate with the perspectives and concerns of individual team members builds rapport and engages them more meaningfully, fostering a stronger connection.
   - Prioritizing their understanding and comfort level with the information being discussed showcases a dedication to meeting their needs, enhancing their involvement in collaborative efforts.
3. **Encouraging Open Dialogue and Inclusivity:**
   - Cultivating an open environment that encourages diverse viewpoints promotes constructive dialogue among colleagues, fostering an atmosphere of mutual respect and understanding.
   - Actively soliciting opinions from various team members

fosters a sense of inclusion, ensuring everyone feels heard and valued in discussions.

4. **Embracing Expertise and Seeking Guidance:**
   - Acknowledging personal limitations and embracing the expertise of others encourages a culture where seeking guidance or clarifications from subject matter experts is embraced, enriching problem-solving and decision-making processes.
   - Encouraging team members to reach out to specialists or experienced colleagues when faced with uncertainties or unfamiliar territory ensures comprehensive and informed decision-making.

5. **Conciseness and Clarity in Communication:**
   - Advocating for concise and clear communication ensures that messages are easy to comprehend and free from unnecessary complexities.
   - Avoiding verbosity or jargon that might confuse or overwhelm listeners promotes clarity, maintaining engagement and facilitating better understanding among team members.

6. **Active Listening and Feedback:**
   - Fostering an environment of active listening during conversations demonstrates respect and validates the viewpoints of others, encouraging reciprocal engagement and mutual understanding.
   - Cultivating a culture of constructive feedback loops ensures that team members feel comfortable providing input to enhance communication practices, fostering continuous improvement.

7. **Adaptability and Flexibility:**
   - Recognizing the diversity among team members and

staying adaptable in communication styles helps adjust approaches to effectively engage with various personalities and working styles.
- Being open to refining communication techniques based on feedback ensures ongoing improvement, ultimately fostering more effective and fruitful exchanges among colleagues.

Effective communication serves as a cornerstone in fostering successful collaborations within organizations. Prioritizing key aspects such as timeliness, audience-centric approaches, open dialogue, recognition of expertise, clarity in communication, active listening and adaptability significantly contributes to cultivating an environment conducive to better communication and improved teamwork.

Timeliness in communication ensures that information is shared promptly, enabling swift decision-making and proactive responses within teams. By acknowledging the importance of delivering information in a timely manner, organizations facilitate a more efficient workflow and bolster their ability to adapt swiftly to changing circumstances.

An audience-centric approach prioritizes understanding the perspectives and concerns of individual team members. Tailoring communication to resonate with their needs and viewpoints fosters a sense of engagement, encouraging active participation and ensuring that everyone feels heard and valued within the team.

Fostering open dialogue creates an inclusive environment that encourages diverse viewpoints and constructive discussions among team members. This approach promotes a culture where ideas are freely shared, leading to innovative solutions and collaborative problem-solving.

Recognizing expertise within the team encourages a culture of seeking guidance and support from subject matter experts. This acknowledgment ensures that teams leverage the knowledge and skills of individuals, enhancing the quality of decision-making and fostering a supportive and collaborative atmosphere.

Clarity in communication is essential to ensure that messages are easily understood and devoid of unnecessary complexity. Clear and concise communication prevents misunderstandings, enabling seamless information exchange and maintaining a shared understanding among team members.

Active listening is a fundamental aspect of effective communication, as it demonstrates respect and validates the perspectives of others. Encouraging active listening within teams fosters an environment of mutual understanding and encourages meaningful engagement during discussions.

Lastly, adaptability in communication styles ensures that teams can effectively interact with diverse personalities and working styles. Being flexible and open to adjusting communication approaches based on the situation and feedback received contributes to more effective exchanges among team members.

By emphasizing these aspects of communication, organizations can establish an environment where effective communication becomes the norm, ultimately leading to improved collaboration, strengthened teamwork and enhanced overall productivity.

BECOMING A BETTER LISTENER

Effective communication indeed surpasses simple verbal exchanges; it encompasses the profound practice of active and attentive listening as a fundamental cornerstone. Active listening, characterized by attentiveness and engagement, forms an indispensable foundation for meaningful and productive interactions. Here, let's explore further insights into the steps that can be taken to strengthen one's capacity for attentive listening:

1. **Clarity in Listening:** beyond the surface-level reception of words, attentive listening involves a commitment to understanding the underlying message. This commitment includes actively seeking clarification when needed, ensuring a comprehensive grasp of the essence and implications of the communicated information. This pursuit of clarity enables precise responses and mitigates the risk of misunderstandings.
2. **Depth in Listening:** attentive listening doesn't merely skim the surface; it delves into the layers of communication, aiming to capture its intricate nuances and diverse viewpoints. This approach involves a genuine curiosity to explore multiple interpretations, creating room for rich and multifaceted exchanges. Such depth allows for a comprehensive understanding that facilitates nuanced and thoughtful responses.
3. **Empathetic Listening:** going beyond the literal words, attentive listening encompasses an empathetic connection to the emotions, intentions and perspectives underlying the communication. It involves recognizing and validating

the feelings and viewpoints expressed by others, fostering trust and creating an environment where individuals feel genuinely heard and valued.
4. **Feedback-Oriented Listening:** attentive listening doesn't conclude with understanding; it actively seeks feedback to ensure alignment and clarity. This approach involves verifying mutual understanding by summarizing or paraphrasing the received information. This feedback loop enhances communication by confirming comprehension and validating the accuracy of the exchanged information.

By embracing and embodying these facets of attentive listening, individuals not only refine their communication skills but also cultivate an environment conducive to robust and meaningful exchanges. Attentive listening serves as a conduit for building connections, resolving conflicts and fostering collaborative endeavours within teams and across organizations. It sets the stage for a more engaged, empathetic and communicative environment where everyone feels valued and understood.

Active listening isn't merely about receiving auditory information; it necessitates deliberate and sustained engagement. Often, external distractions disrupt the depth of understanding during conversations, causing a divergence between mere auditory reception and comprehensive comprehension. The rapidity of human thought processes frequently leads to premature assumptions and mental tangents, impacting the quality of interactions.

1. **Cultivating Mindful Presence:** active listening goes beyond hearing—it's about being fully present. Cultivating mindfulness aids in resisting external distractions that might infiltrate conversations. Techniques such as deep

breathing or mental grounding serve as anchors amid the chaos of surrounding stimuli, fostering better focus and engagement.

2. **Overcoming Mental Drift:** human thoughts tend to move swiftly, leading to premature assumptions or mental tangents during conversations. To counter this, cultivating self-awareness becomes crucial. Recognizing when the mind starts to wander allows for intentional redirection of attention back to the speaker's words, ensuring a deeper level of understanding.
3. **Strategies for Engagement:** active listening requires conscious effort to engage with the speaker actively. Techniques like paraphrasing or summarizing key points demonstrate active involvement, ensuring not only comprehension but also reassuring the speaker of being heard and understood.
4. **Utilizing Non-Verbal Communication:** beyond words, non-verbal cues significantly contribute to active listening. Maintaining eye contact, nodding in agreement, or using affirmative gestures solidify connections and convey genuine interest, affirming the speaker's importance in the conversation.
5. **Effective Questioning:** thoughtful questioning without interrupting the speaker's flow is a skillful aspect of active listening. It involves curiosity and the intention to delve deeper into the speaker's thoughts, clarifying ambiguities without disrupting their narrative, fostering a more in-depth understanding.
6. **Empathy and Emotional Understanding:** understanding emotions adds depth to active listening. It's about sensing the emotional tone, empathizing with the speaker's feelings

and acknowledging their perspective. This emotional understanding deepens connections and enriches comprehension.
7. **Adaptability and Flexibility:** active listening isn't a one-size-fits-all approach. Adapting techniques to different personalities and situations is crucial. Some might prefer direct engagement, while others might require subtler forms of validation, showcasing the importance of adapting to individual preferences.
8. **Continuous Practice and Feedback:** developing active listening skills is an ongoing journey. Regular practice, reflection and seeking feedback refine these skills over time. Embracing feedback allows for adjustments and continual improvement in active listening abilities.
9. **Creating a Supportive Environment:** valuing active listening fosters reciprocal behaviour. When everyone in a conversation practices active listening, it establishes a culture of mutual respect and understanding, enhancing overall communication dynamics.
10. **Cognitive and Emotional Load Management:** recognizing that active listening demands cognitive and emotional investment is pivotal. Understanding personal thresholds for managing these loads ensures sustained and effective listening over time, avoiding burnout or exhaustion.

In essence, active listening is a multifaceted skill that goes beyond auditory reception—it's about understanding and empathizing with the speaker. It necessitates mental focus, emotional intelligence and deliberate engagement to forge meaningful connections and enhance comprehension.

Intentional dedication to honing listening skills reaps

extensive benefits that span various facets of personal and professional life. Consistent practice in this area goes beyond skill refinement; it becomes a transformative journey that enriches interactions, fosters deeper connections and propels both individual growth and collaborative success.

In the context of relationships, whether personal or professional, adept listening forms the bedrock of strong rapport. By cultivating attentive listening skills, individuals foster connections that transcend the surface level, nurturing trust, comprehension and empathy in their interactions.

In professional settings, refined listening proficiency is a catalyst for productivity, innovation and effective collaboration. Engaging actively in discussions, grasping subtleties in perspectives and comprehending colleagues' viewpoints empower individuals to navigate complexities, resolve conflicts and contribute meaningfully to collective objectives. This elevated listening ability becomes pivotal in harmonizing teams, fostering creativity and unlocking the collective intelligence within.

Moreover, the benefits of attentive listening extend beyond interpersonal dynamics, influencing personal growth and self-awareness. Immersing oneself in others' narratives concurrently fosters a deeper understanding of one's thought processes and biases. This introspective journey amplifies emotional intelligence and nurtures self-reflection, shaping a more empathetic and inclusive individual, thereby contributing positively to society.

Ultimately, the deliberate pursuit of refining listening skills is an investment that enhances the depth and quality of interactions. It weaves a tapestry of understanding, productivity, and enriched human connections that reverberate across various spheres of life, elevating relationships, professional accomplishments and personal development.

MASTERING THE ART OF EFFECTIVE QUESTIONING

The art of questioning is a profound and impactful skill that complements attentive listening in communication. Crafted thoughtfully, questions act as keys unlocking a wealth of insights and fostering deeper understanding between communicators.

1. **Precision in Inquiry:** thoughtful questions tailored to specific contexts unveil layers of information, enriching understanding and nurturing insightful conversations.
2. **Building Bridges of Understanding:** well-constructed questions promote a profound comprehension of subjects, encouraging convergence of diverse viewpoints and mutual understanding.
3. **Empowering Others' Voices:** questions validate experiences and perspectives, fostering inclusivity and respect for diverse viewpoints within dialogue.
4. **Questioning and Empathetic Listening:** thoughtful questions demonstrate empathy, signaling a commitment not just to hearing but comprehending others' perspectives, nurturing connections.
5. **Quality of Decisions and Information:** thoughtful questioning gathers comprehensive data crucial for informed decisions, preventing skewed outcomes due to inaccurate or insufficient information.
6. **Critical Thinking and Problem Solving:** questions catalyze critical thinking, challenging assumptions and fostering innovative solutions, promoting a problem-solving mindset.
7. **Adaptability and Learning:** embracing questioning nurtures adaptability, fueling a continuous cycle of learning

and exploration of the unknown.
8. **Facilitating Growth and Progress:** questions drive personal development and societal progress, fueling curiosity and propelling advancement across various domains.

Questioning isn't solely about seeking information; it's a catalyst for understanding, diverse perspectives, informed decision-making, and progress. A well-crafted question initiates a chain reaction of discovery and growth, shaping not only present conversations but also future endeavours.

> *'Ninety-nine percent of failures come from people who have the habit of making excuses.'*
>
> —GEORGE WASHINGTON CARVER

MASTERING THE ART OF CREATIVE CRITICISM

Mastering the art of creative criticism is a multifaceted endeavour, intricately weaving insight and empathy into the fabric of feedback delivery. It's not solely about pinpointing flaws but delving into the nuances that contribute to them. The process demands a keen eye for detail, a thoughtful analysis and a compassionate approach. Effective criticism is an art that requires careful observation, thorough assessment, and the articulation of feedback in a manner that encourages growth while maintaining a supportive and constructive tone. It's about presenting actionable suggestions for improvement while highlighting strengths, fostering an environment that empowers individuals rather than demoralizing them. Achieving mastery in this delicate art form involves transforming critique into a springboard for progress, instilling a proactive mindset for change and nurturing a culture that values continuous growth and resilience in the face of adversity.

1. **Investigating Root Causes:** delving deeper to understand the underlying reasons behind performance issues is akin to exploring the unseen currents beneath the surface. It involves a meticulous examination that seeks to unearth the complexities contributing to the situation. This depth of understanding informs a critique that is not just comprehensive but also empathetic, addressing the core issues rather than merely their manifestations.
2. **Tailored Suggestions for Growth:** offering pathways for improvement is akin to providing a roadmap through the maze of challenges. These suggestions are not just generic fixes but tailored solutions that align with the specific context. Crafting these recommendations in a supportive and encouraging manner ensures they are perceived as opportunities for advancement rather than fault-finding.
3. **Nurturing Positivity:** maintaining an optimistic disposition while addressing challenges involves a tightrope walk between acknowledging existing hurdles and fostering hope for improvement. It's about creating a narrative that acknowledges difficulties without overshadowing the potential for growth. This positive tone in critiques creates an atmosphere where individuals are inspired to overcome obstacles proactively.
4. **Proactive Problem-Solving:** effective critique is not a passive act; it's a call to action. It's not merely pointing out cracks in the system but actively engaging in mending them. Encouraging a proactive approach involves not just identifying problems but participating in the quest for viable

solutions. This proactive stance bridges the gap between identifying issues and instigating constructive changes.
5. **Balanced Feedback:** an adept critic doesn't just highlight weaknesses; they shine a light on strengths too. Balancing feedback by acknowledging positives alongside areas for development cultivates a well-rounded perspective. This approach fosters a culture that values growth rather than dwelling on faults, nurturing an environment where improvements are celebrated.
6. **Transforming Critique into Motivation:** critique, when presented constructively, becomes a potent motivator. Encouraging individuals to view criticism as a catalyst for positive change empowers them to take charge of their growth journey. Motivation serves as the fuel that propels individuals to initiate transformative actions, leading to tangible improvements.
7. **Advocating Innovation and Change:** elevating from identifying problems to actively advocating innovative solutions positions one as a change agent. It's not about dwelling on issues but steering conversations toward constructive change. This proactive stance creates a ripple effect, inspiring others to engage in transformative actions.
8. **Building a Reputation for Positivity:** being recognized as a solutions-driven, positive contributor creates a reputation that precedes interactions. This reputation establishes one as a collaborator rather than a critic, opening doors for partnerships and collaborative efforts aimed at progress.
9. **Cultivating an Atmosphere of Development:** embracing a mindset that promotes solutions and positive change nurtures an ecosystem that fosters growth. It sets the

stage for a culture where challenges are viewed as stepping stones, encouraging progress on both personal and collective levels.

In essence, effective critique transcends the act of pointing out flaws; it's about providing tailor-made suggestions, maintaining a positive narrative and actively engaging in the quest for solutions. This approach transforms criticism into a catalyst for growth, positioning individuals as champions of positive change within their spheres of influence.

TEAMING

> *'The essence of a team is common commitment. Without it, the members of a group perform as individuals; with it they become a powerful unit for collective performance.'*
>
> —ARTHUR R. PELL

Navigating the intricacies of team dynamics involves traversing a multifaceted landscape brimming with challenges and opportunities. Your approach to collaboration with fellow team members holds the power to shape not only your personal demeanour but also the very fabric of the team's ambiance and collective productivity.

At the core of a successful team lies a culture that doesn't just embrace but actively celebrates innovative thinking. This foundational ethos extends beyond the mere conception of novel ideas; it instils an unwavering commitment essential for translating these visionary concepts into tangible results within the organizational context. It's about cultivating an environment that not only encourages creative thought but also channels that creativity into practical solutions, propelling the team toward its goals.

The essence of triumphant teams lies in their active engagement in the daily decision-making processes, resulting in tangible contributions that reflect the collaborative efforts. These outcomes act as visible markers of the team's collective endeavours, demonstrating the impact of collaborative work. Actively involving team members in decision-making not only fosters a sense of ownership but also ensures that a diverse array of perspectives is considered, leading to more comprehensive and well-informed choices.

Furthermore, recognizing exceptional performances within the team serves as more than just a motivational tool; it's a reinforcement of an appreciative culture. Acknowledging outstanding contributions not only uplifts individuals but also nurtures a positive feedback loop within the team. This loop, in turn, boosts team morale and productivity, creating an environment where appreciation fuels a continuous cycle of exceptional performance.

In essence, the success of a team isn't solely defined by the generation of creative ideas; it's about embedding an ethos that encourages innovation and channels it into actionable outcomes. It's about involving everyone in decision-making, witnessing tangible results and fostering a culture that appreciates and celebrates exceptional efforts, driving the team towards collective success.

The landscape of teamwork is not merely about overcoming obstacles; it's also about cultivating an environment that places a premium on innovation, active participation, visible achievements and the celebration of excellence. It's about nurturing a culture where every team member feels empowered to contribute, creating a collective synergy that drives the team toward achieving its goals and attaining success.

Assessing your role as a leader within a team is a pivotal and multi-layered process. It involves a comprehensive understanding of the specific traits that hold paramount importance in effective leadership. Valuable insights derived from an extensive study encompassing over 5,000 employees have illuminated perceptions regarding the foundational qualities of effective leadership. This comprehensive study, spanning diverse industries, demographics and organizational structures, revealed a consensus on ten qualities universally regarded as essential for effective team leadership. These qualities emerged as undeniable benchmarks of successful leadership, transcending barriers such as gender, age, industry size and corporate culture.

In this comprehensive assessment, the aim is to delve deep into these critical qualities, dissecting and understanding their intricacies to better assess their presence within one's own leadership approach. Conducting a meticulous evaluation of each aspect, utilizing a scale like 'S' for Strong, 'A' for Average, or 'W' for Weak, becomes a practical tool for self-assessment against these identified traits. Furthermore, soliciting evaluations from five individuals familiar with your work, using the same criteria, adds an additional layer to this introspective process. Their varied perspectives contribute to a more comprehensive and holistic self-assessment, offering diverse insights into your leadership style and its alignment with the identified essential qualities.

1. _____ Offering precise directives
2. _____ Cultivating transparent and reciprocal communication
3. _____ Willingness to mentor and uplift team members

4. _____ Dispensing fair and unbiased recognition
5. _____ Establishing ongoing checks and balances
6. _____ Strategically staffing the organization with the right personnel
7. _____ Understanding the financial implications of decisions
8. _____ Fostering innovation and embracing new concepts
9. _____ Making decisive resolutions when necessary
10. _____ Consistently maintaining high levels of integrity

When assessing oneself in comparison to external evaluations, it's apparent that perceptions can widely differ. The discrepancy between one's self-perception and how others perceive them often unravels fascinating insights. There are instances where what might be internally regarded as adept diplomacy could, from an external standpoint, be construed as a hint of patronization. Similarly, the cautiousness exercised in decision-making, seen from one's viewpoint as thoroughness and prudence, might be misinterpreted by others as indecisiveness, leading to divergent perceptions and potential misjudgements.

These disparities in perception become starkly apparent when self-awareness is unveiled only upon receiving explicit feedback. For instance, the recognition of being perceived as abrasive can be surprising when confronted with direct feedback about one's demeanour or behaviour. These disparities emphasize the intricate nature of interpersonal dynamics, revealing how others interpret one's actions and intentions.

Addressing identified weaknesses stemming from these contrasts becomes imperative. For instance, comprehending that perceived caution might inadvertently convey indecisiveness prompts a revaluation of decision-making approaches. This involves a conscious effort to strike a balance between thoroughness and timeliness, ensuring decisions are well-informed yet efficiently made. It calls for a recalibration of one's approach, aligning it more closely with external expectations while retaining authenticity and personal integrity. This process of self-reflection and adjustment is crucial for enhancing interpersonal interactions and aligning perceptions with intentions.

Systematically addressing these identified weaknesses becomes an avenue to bridge the gap between self-perception and external assessments. This multifaceted approach involves a continuous process of introspection, actively seeking and embracing feedback and a resolute commitment to evolving and refining behaviours to better align with the desired perceptions. This iterative journey of improvement extends beyond mere rectification of perceived weaknesses; it fosters a deeper understanding of how one's actions are perceived and interpreted by others. This understanding forms the bedrock of more effective and harmonious interpersonal interactions, laying the groundwork for enhanced collaboration and positive relationships within various spheres.

DEVELOPING YOUR INTERPERSONAL RELATIONSHIPS

Establishing and nurturing positive relationships within a professional environment is not only fundamental but also transformative in shaping a constructive and supportive workspace. It's undeniably a cornerstone for influencing others in a positive manner and fostering a culture steeped in collaboration and mutual respect.

The reflective exercise comprising the set of ten questions serves as an invaluable tool for self-assessment. It aims not just for a perfunctory evaluation but a deeper introspection into the impact one's actions and demeanour have on the office environment. Responding candidly with a simple 'yes' or 'no' to these questions sets the stage for an honest evaluation, circumventing any personal biases or the inclination to rationalize behaviours.

This exercise underscores an essential reality: while we might be well-versed in the motivations and circumstances that drive our actions, others often judge and perceive us solely based on the impact of these actions. By engaging in this reflective process, we bridge the chasm between our intentions and how these intentions are perceived by our colleagues.

Beyond individual intentions lies the recognition that our actions, despite the best of intentions, might not always translate into the desired impact. This reflective self-assessment acts as a catalyst for heightened awareness, fostering an acute realization of the ripple effects our behaviours cast on the office ambiance, team dynamics, and the fabric of individual relationships. It's an invitation to a more mindful approach, beckoning us to delve deeper into how our mere presence shapes the workplace atmosphere and, by extension, the experiences of those around us.

The candid answers to these questions prompt us to engage in productive self-reflection and take necessary steps forward. This exercise underscores the importance of humility, acknowledging that personal development frequently arises from recognizing areas where we can enhance our approach. Through an objective evaluation of our impact on the office environment, we unlock opportunities to improve connections, refine communication methods, and better align our actions with the impact we aim to achieve. In essence, this self-assessment goes beyond affirming positive influence; it's about pinpointing areas for development and actively striving to become a more positive and influential presence in the workplace.

Do you tend to be condescendingly critical? When discussing others within the organization, do you exhibit a desire to "straighten them out"?

Yes _____ No _____

Do you feel the need for absolute control? Is it necessary for almost everything to obtain your approval?
Yes _____ No _____

During meetings, do your comments consume a disproportionate amount of time?
Yes _____ No _____

Are you quick to launch attacks?
Yes _____ No _____

Do you hesitate to grant others the same privileges or benefits that you enjoy?
Yes _____ No _____

When conversing, do you frequently use the word "I"?
Yes _____ No _____

Are you admired by others primarily due to your strength, capability, position, or status?
Yes _____ No _____

Do people perceive you as cold and distant, despite your desire for them to like you?
Yes _____ No _____

Do you consider yourself more competent than your peers or even your boss? Does your behaviour reflect this belief?
Yes _____ No _____

Do you derive satisfaction from acquiring symbols of status and power?

Yes _____ No _____

Upon reviewing the assessment outcomes, if your responses lean towards three to five "yes" answers, it could signal a potential perception of your behaviour being abrasive. This flags a need for introspection and potential adjustments in your approach to interpersonal interactions. However, if the assessment reveals six or more "yes" answers, it might indicate a more significant issue that requires immediate attention and remedial action.

Understanding how your behaviour impacts colleagues' morale is pivotal for fostering a conducive work environment. If the assessment points to potential issues, examining your attitude and conduct becomes a crucial starting point. This self-reflection aims not just at acknowledging but also at comprehending the potential implications of one's actions and their effects on colleagues' perceptions.

The involvement of executive coaches signifies a commitment to continuous improvement and underscores the acknowledgment that creating a positive work environment requires active participation and self-reflection. It's a strategic investment in personal growth and professional development, paving the way for a more harmonious and productive workplace culture. By addressing potential issues highlighted by the assessment and seeking guidance where necessary, individuals can bridge gaps in perception, refine their approach, and contribute to a more positive and cohesive work environment.

IMPROVING MORALE

The elevation of morale isn't a mere bestowment; it flourishes in an environment where individuals confidently articulate their career aspirations, where their training needs find resolution, and where assertiveness is not only welcomed but embraced. Such an atmosphere emerges from a collaborative partnership between managers and employees, where empowerment acts as the driving force for augmenting morale.

When individuals possess the belief in their capacity to initiate change, wield control over their work, and actively engage in decision-making processes, the visible enhancement in morale becomes apparent.

1. **Fostering Career Aspirations:** Elevating morale intertwines deeply with creating an environment where individuals feel empowered to express and pursue their career aspirations. This entails establishing open communication channels where employees confidently voice their professional goals, enabling managers to align organizational opportunities with individual ambitions effectively.
2. **Addressing Training Needs:** Recognizing and attending to training needs stands as a crucial pillar. It showcases organizational dedication to employee growth and development, fostering a sense of investment in their skill enhancement. Providing learning opportunities not only amplifies competence but also significantly contributes to morale-boosting efforts.

3. **Embracing Assertiveness:** A culture that embraces assertiveness empowers individuals to voice opinions, challenge norms, and contribute substantially to discussions. Encouraging and valuing assertiveness nurtures an environment where diverse perspectives are prized, exerting a positive influence on morale.
4. **Manager-Employee Collaboration:** Morale elevation is a joint effort between managers and employees. Managers play a pivotal role in nurturing an environment conducive to boosting morale. They serve as facilitators, supporting and enabling the growth and aspirations of their team members.
5. **Empowerment as a Driving Force:** Empowering individuals acts as a catalyst for enhancing morale. When employees feel empowered, they exhibit heightened confidence in initiating actions, assuming control over their work, and actively engaging in decision-making processes.
6. **Confidence in Action and Autonomy:** Morale thrives when individuals believe in their ability to initiate change and exercise control over their work. Empowering employees with autonomy and decision-making authority not only elevates morale but also fosters a sense of ownership and accountability.
7. **Active Involvement in Decision-Making:** Involving employees in decision-making processes profoundly impacts morale. It communicates trust and respect for their expertise, resulting in increased engagement, satisfaction, and a stronger sense of belonging within the organization.
8. **Tangible Results of Empowerment:** Empowerment generates palpable shifts in morale. There's a noticeable surge in enthusiasm, motivation, and commitment to achieving organizational goals.

9. **Cultivating a Positive Work Environment:** The amalgamation of supporting career aspirations, addressing training needs, embracing assertiveness, fostering collaboration, and empowerment converges in cultivating a positive work environment that substantially raises morale.
10. **Enduring Impact:** Elevating morale isn't a quick fix; it's a continual process requiring ongoing commitment and effort. Sustained empowerment and support pave the path for enduring positive morale, contributing to a thriving and resilient organizational culture.

CHANGE BEFORE YOU MUST

Embracing change before it becomes an urgent demand is indeed a formidable skill to develop. It necessitates a proactive mindset and an openness to transformation, both of which require deliberate cultivation. However, nurturing a positive outlook has the potential to profoundly reshape how one perceives and navigates through change. It's about fostering a mindset that not only welcomes evolution but also views it as an avenue for personal and professional growth rather than a disruptive force. This shift in perspective, while challenging, demands a conscious effort to step outside comfort zones and break away from familiar routines. Yet, embracing a positive stance stands as a powerful strategy to mitigate the inherent difficulties associated with change.

Adopting a positive outlook equips individuals with resilience and adaptability in the face of change. It acknowledges change as an inevitable aspect of life and work and, by embracing it proactively, helps mitigate its disruptive effects. This positive stance creates an environment characterized by readiness and flexibility, enabling individuals to respond to new circumstances with agility and innovative solutions.

However, it's essential to recognize that embracing change positively doesn't erase its challenges or complexities. It's an ongoing process that demands patience, persistence, and a willingness to adapt. Yet, by nurturing this outlook, individuals establish the groundwork for a more constructive and empowered response to change, fostering an environment conducive to innovation, growth, and success amid constantly evolving landscapes.

Consider these comprehensive steps as a roadmap to propel your personal and professional growth:

1. **Analyse Your Position Objectively:** Reflect deeply on your current state and future paths to gain clarity for strategic decisions.
2. **Anticipate Challenges and Solutions:** Identify looming threats and preemptively devise strategies to navigate uncertainties and build resilience.
3. **Set Ambitious Goals:** Challenge yourself with extraordinary objectives for continuous growth and distinction.
4. **Leverage Strengths for Versatility:** Use your strengths to create diverse opportunities, allowing exploration in multiple arenas.
5. **Plan with Adaptability:** Develop flexible plans with contingency strategies for evolving circumstances and swift pivots.
6. **Foster Continuous Learning:** Commit to ongoing skill development and acquiring new knowledge for agile readiness.

7. **Network for Diverse Perspectives:** Engage in collaborations that broaden perspectives and create innovative solutions.
8. **Embrace Resilience and Adaptation:** Embody adaptability as a strength to navigate challenges and thrive in dynamic environments.

Individuals who diligently strategize and prepare stand out among their peers. Their proactive approach involves careful planning, setting clear objectives, and comprehensive preparation, guiding them toward success.

This proactive mindset goes beyond planning; it involves analysis, foresight, and preparing for challenges. This forward-thinking approach enables them to anticipate hurdles, create contingency plans, and respond swiftly in complex or changing environments.

Investing in meticulous preparation instills confidence. These individuals approach challenges with assurance, armed with well-thought-out plans and a deep understanding of their surroundings. This readiness empowers them to navigate uncertainties with poise and seize opportunities confidently.

To preemptively prevent unexpected setbacks:

1. **Expertise Refinement:** Invest time and effort in refining your specialized knowledge and skills within your field. Continuous learning and staying updated with the latest trends and innovations are pivotal for staying ahead in your domain.
2. **Resource Familiarization:** Identify crucial resources vital to your success and become well-acquainted with their accessibility and potential applications. These resources span

beyond tangible assets, encompassing networks, mentors, and knowledge repositories.
3. **Resource Optimization:** Once identified, maximize the use of these resources to yield optimal benefits and outcomes. Effective utilization ensures efficiency and magnifies the impact of your endeavours.
4. **Progress Tracking:** Set up an objective tracking system to consistently monitor and evaluate progress. Clear metrics, milestones, and checkpoints enable the adjustment of strategies as needed.
5. **Data-Driven Outlook:** Cultivate a pragmatic view of the future based on factual information and data-driven insights rather than subjective opinions. This forms a robust basis for strategic decision-making.
6. **Efficient Time Management:** Employ smart time management strategies to enhance productivity. Prioritize tasks, allocate time wisely, and minimize distractions to streamline workflow.
7. **Self-Discipline:** Practice unwavering self-discipline by setting boundaries, adhering to schedules, and maintaining consistent efforts and behaviours.
8. **Positive Environment:** Surround yourself with positivity and constructive influences while distancing from negativity. A supportive network aids focus and motivation towards your objectives.
9. **Adaptability:** Foster adaptability while preparing meticulously. Being open to adjusting strategies based on evolving circumstances ensures resilience in navigating challenges.
10. **Continuous Improvement:** Regularly evaluate and adjust your strategies, embracing a mindset of continuous

improvement. Seek feedback and refine approaches based on lessons learned and changing dynamics.

Meticulous planning is key for success, providing an edge and instilling a mindset of preparation, adaptability, and resilience, vital in today's dynamic landscape.

Expanding your knowledge base is foundational for strategic success. Actively learning about emerging trends and innovations empowers informed decisions, adaptation, and seizing opportunities.

Leveraging this knowledge fortifies strategic approaches, ensuring they align with current trends. Integrating insights into planning creates a resilient framework that anticipates and responds to change.

Embracing change proactively is an active engagement, viewing it as an opportunity. This mindset cultivates flexibility, resilience, and agility, enabling you to navigate uncertainties and capitalize on emerging opportunities.

By continuously learning, fortifying strategies with innovative approaches, and proactively adapting to change, you create an environment primed not only for positive morale but also for exceptional success in professional endeavours.

LEVERAGE YOUR ABILITIES

'More failure results from indecision than wrong choices.'

When faced with a pivotal moment demanding a shift in direction, individuals often encounter diverse catalysts driving this change. Whether it's reaching the peak of personal growth, the allure of fresh opportunities, or a sense of weariness from routine, embracing change requires a strategic approach. Here are five key considerations:

1. **Embracing Challenges and Feedback:** Expect obstacles and actively seek feedback and critique. Developing resilience in the face of challenges empowers you to find innovative solutions and navigate transitions more effectively.
2. **Managing Expectations and Commitment:** Recognize that significant progress resulting from a new beginning takes time. Maintain commitment and focus on long-term goals while appreciating the small steps toward achievement.
3. **Rejecting Mediocrity:** Avoid settling for roles that don't align with your potential. Pursue positions allowing you to creatively blend your diverse skill set, leveraging strengths harmoniously. Aim for roles that ignite passion and purpose.
4. **Continuous Learning and Flexibility:** Embrace a growth mindset by consistently expanding your knowledge. Stay adaptable and open to change as opportunities evolve, demanding a flexible approach.
5. **Networking and Collaboration:** Engage in diverse networks and collaborative efforts. Building connections opens up new perspectives, opportunities, and potential partnerships that enrich the journey through transition.

Incorporating these strategies into your approach to change enables more effective navigation through transitions, leveraging strengths, and embracing new growth and fulfillment opportunities.

Charles Kettering, a luminary akin to Thomas Edison, embodies the self-made inventor and industrial tycoon archetype. His legacy boasts 200+ patents, notably the electronic self-starter, now a car engine staple. Beyond this, his impact spans diesel engines, anti-knock gas, home AC, and fast-drying car paint.

His unconventional education challenged norms, believing traditional paths hindered innovation. Eyestrain led to a unique method—relying on others to read aloud, honing his ability to visualize concepts internally, vital to his inventiveness. Overcoming visual challenges catalyzed his creativity, sparking unparalleled achievements.

Some argue Kettering excelled because of, not despite, his vision issues. His determination to surpass hurdles gave him a unique perspective, propelling his genius. His story shows adversity fuels extraordinary creativity and success.

Embracing change, leveraging strengths, and fostering resilience empower individuals through transitions. Learning from trailblazers like Kettering guides us in facing change with determination, enabling personal growth and innovative thinking in our journey.

AVOID DOUBTERS

'Optimists see possibilities. Pessimists refuse to look.'

Influential figures wield immense power over our beliefs and mindset. Those who propagate a narrative of impossibility risk infecting us with skepticism. Doubters and pessimists, staunch in their convictions about what can't be done, often face stagnation or regression. To foster growth, it's vital to distance from these "mildewed" individuals—metaphorically tainted by prolonged darkness—if one believes in potential progress.

In 1920, Robert Goddard, a Clark University physics professor, published a groundbreaking paper envisioning rockets capable of reaching the moon. The idea faced widespread skepticism. Despite dismissals and scorn, Goddard boldly held onto his vision, asserting, "Every vision is a joke until the first person accomplishes it."

Goddard focused on propellants suitable for space exploration, experimenting with liquid hydrogen and liquid oxygen. In 1926, he launched a 10-foot rocket, hitting 60 mph for 2.5 seconds at an altitude of 41 feet. Realizing the challenge ahead—breaking free from Earth's gravity—he intensified his work in New Mexico, testing rockets up to 18 feet long. Some surpassed the speed of sound, using innovative fin-stabilized steering that shaped future designs.

During World War II, Goddard's work influenced cutting-edge aircraft. By his death in 1945, he held 214 patents, solidifying his legacy as the father of modern rocketry. His dedication triumphed over skepticism, establishing him as a pioneer in interstellar exploration.

LEAN FORWARD AND DON'T LOOK BACK

In the unforgiving theater of war, leadership operates on a knife's edge. Mistakes lead to defeat. Historical military leaders like Sun Tzu, Napoleon, and Patton offer timeless lessons not just in strategy but also in personal growth. Their tales reveal profound insights into leadership, resilience, and human nature under extreme pressure.

These narratives encompass much more than conquests and defeats. They teach the art of deception, logistics mastery, motivation, and adaptability—lessons that transcend time and circumstance.

In the crucible of war, decisions shape history. The annals of military command are a rich source of wisdom, not only for strategists but also for anyone navigating life's complexities with purpose and wisdom.

Ulysses S. Grant earned President Lincoln's admiration for his dedication to fighting, immortalizing their camaraderie with witty remarks. General Sherman acknowledged Grant's unparalleled resilience, stating that while he might surpass Grant in strategy and logistics, Grant's unwavering persistence was unmatched.

Grant's legacy goes beyond tactical genius—it embodies resilience in the face of adversity, inspiring not just military minds but anyone facing life's challenges. His perseverance teaches an enduring lesson in human resilience and the determination to overcome obstacles.

Hannibal's audacious trek through the Alps with elephants epitomizes his unwavering determination. Despite skepticism, he pushed forward, famously stating, "We shall discover a path or forge one." His relentless commitment to his vision symbolizes human tenacity and the pursuit of the seemingly impossible.

Hannibal's resolve in navigating the Alps stands as an enduring example of human determination. His ability to face skepticism and adversity with unwavering determination serves as an inspiration—a timeless lesson in the resilience of the human spirit.

Amidst the chaos of the Battle of Mobile Bay in 1864, **Admiral David Farragut** faced a pivotal moment. His flagship was destroyed, leading some officers to advise retreat. Unwavering, Farragut took command, climbed his damaged ship's rigging, and famously declared, "Damn the torpedoes! Full speed ahead!" This resolute act epitomized courage and leadership under fire, showcasing Farragut's unwavering determination and valor in the face of imminent danger, a testament to the resilience of true leadership amidst uncertainty.

*'Courageous people look fear in the face and say,
"Bring it on!"'*

Napoleon Bonaparte revealed the secret behind his strategic brilliance, emphasizing that his appearance of perpetual readiness wasn't spontaneous genius but the result of thorough preparation and contemplation. He invested extensive time in forecasting potential outcomes and deep meditation, laying the foundation for his foresight in navigating uncertain circumstances. This insight underscores the importance of diligent contemplation and groundwork in fostering readiness amidst uncertainty.

'You lead not by what you say, but by what you do.'

The stories of these historic leaders echo timelessly, immortalizing their unwavering spirits that faced impossible odds without hesitation. Their resolve, determination, and audacity stand as guiding lights for personal and professional growth. These accounts hold invaluable lessons, revealing insights into resilience, fortitude, and unwavering pursuit despite obstacles. Their legacies offer timeless guidance for navigating life's complexities. Embracing their examples reveals a well of wisdom beyond time and circumstance, illustrating the human capacity for resilience and fortitude in conquering challenges on the path to growth and success.

10

POSITIVE ATTITUDE— THE KEY TO SUCCESS

'Things turn out best for the people who make the best of the way things turn out.'

—JOHN WOODEN

A positive attitude not only shapes success but also shields against burnout and fuels skill growth. It's the cornerstone for triumph in both life and work. Appreciating existing blessings and embracing ambition, whether in business or service, drives success. Achieving goals requires unwavering commitment and individual prowess, leading from acceptability to excellence through dedication and hard work.

Achieving excellence often requires traversing a challenging path of learning and growth, where experience shapes potential into skill. To maximize the chances of turning hard work into success, certain essential personal attributes play a pivotal role:

1. Self-esteem forms the foundation for achieving aspirations, empowering individuals to navigate life's opportunities with confidence and control.

2. Responsibility embodies personal agency, embracing the accountability for shaping one's destiny through triumphs and trials.
3. Optimism fuels success, driven by an unwavering belief in potential amidst uncertain circumstances, fostering self-assurance and diligent effort.
4. Steady Progress marks deliberate advancement, aligning present actions with future goals to propel success steadily forward.
5. Imagination breeds innovation, cultivating new ideas and possibilities, transcending limits to chart unconventional paths.
6. Awareness, fueled by curiosity, keeps watch for new opportunities, ready to seize fleeting chances.
7. Creativity sparks transformation, challenging norms, and exploring diverse perspectives for innovation and evolution.

> *'Always bear in mind that your own resolution to succeed is more important than any other one thing.'*
>
> —ABRAHAM LINCOLN

CRITERIA FOR SUCCESSFUL LEADERS

Lee Iacocca's leadership at Chrysler epitomized a willingness to confront failure in pursuit of monumental triumphs. His pragmatic leadership, vividly expressed through his team, encapsulated these characteristics:

1. Risk-Taking Mavericks: Fearless innovators unafraid to pursue uncharted paths, willing to risk their standing for pioneering projects.

2. **Controlled Workaholics:** Passion-driven achievers who transcend traditional work hours, finding reward in accomplishment over time spent.
3. **Honest Communicators:** Bold and sincere in expressing their convictions, fostering open and constructive dialogue.
4. **Fearless Delegators:** Courageous leaders who trust their team, promoting autonomy and accountability for success or failure.
5. **Practical Planners:** Visionaries with a systematic approach, prioritizing tasks and plotting a comprehensive roadmap for success.
6. **Tough-Minded Decision-Makers:** Resolute in making difficult choices for the collective good, prioritizing efficiency over sentimentality.
7. **Dreamers with Common Sense:** Balancing visionary ideas with practical outcomes, focusing on achievable results.
8. **Sacrificial Performers:** Dedicated, energetic individuals who exceed expectations, inspiring others through their unwavering commitment.

THE ATTRIBUTES OF WINNERS

Winners excel in interpersonal dynamics by anchoring their relationships on four crucial principles:

1. **Uncovering Motivational Triggers:** They believe everyone holds unique motivational keys. Managers decode these triggers, unlocking potential and enthusiasm for a more engaged workforce.
2. **Tapping Intrinsic Motivations:** Winners understand personal aspirations drive individuals. They align these motivations with organizational goals, fostering

a harmonious synergy between personal desires and professional tasks.
3. Addressing Individual Concerns: Acknowledging and integrating personal concerns into tasks fosters inclusivity and commitment within the team, creating a more considerate environment.
4. Cultivating Effective Communication: They create an open dialogue, bridging the gap between leadership goals and individual motivations, nurturing trust and understanding within the organization.

These winners recognize the complexity of motivation, aspirations, and empathetic communication. They weave these elements together, building relationships founded on respect, understanding, and a collective drive toward shared objectives.

Moreover, they grasp two critical notions:

1. Balancing Strengths: Overemphasizing strengths, like an obsession with punctuality, can overshadow the value of contributions. Leaders avoid favouring a single trait at the expense of substance and ideas.
2. Internal Motivation: Effective leaders don't rely solely on external rewards. They cultivate an environment where autonomy and empowerment inspire self-driven action, fostering a culture of initiative and progress.

ENTHUSIASM IS CONTAGIOUS

Enthusiasm acts as a powerful force shaping environments, as exemplified by Tommy Lasorda, the vibrant manager of the Los Angeles Dodgers. He emphasizes that a leader's attitude is contagious, setting the tone for their team's collective mindset.

Lasorda's analogy vividly highlights how a leader's demeanour influences team morale, fostering an atmosphere either of despondency or of energy and optimism.

His insights extend beyond attitude, emphasizing the reciprocal nature of loyalty in organizations. Lasorda sees loyalty as a bond forged by mutual dedication and appreciation. He stresses the connection between cultivating a deep love for work and the resulting pride that drives outstanding performance. His reflections prompt us to consider the rarity of individuals passionately devoted to their organizations even beyond their lifetimes, emphasizing the need to nurture loyalty and dedication in the workplace.

Lasorda's wisdom underscores the link between a leader's enthusiasm and the organizational ethos. Leaders who embody positivity wield an influential power that shapes collective morale and productivity. Moreover, his focus on reciprocal loyalty underscores the importance of fostering a workplace culture where dedication, pride, and love for work thrive, creating an environment where loyalty and exceptional performance are fundamental to success.

> *'You are as young as your faith*
> *As old as your doubts*
> *As young as your self confidence*
> *As old as your fears*
> *As young as your hope*
> *As old as your despair.*
> *Years may wrinkle the skin*
> *But to give up enthusiasm*
> *Wrinkles the soul.'*
>
> —SAMUEL ULLMAN

Effective leadership hinges on attitude, driving organizational progress. Leaders who grasp this correlation propel their teams forward, fostering a collective vision of success:

- They nurture a culture where assisting team members reciprocates, creating a collaborative environment. Obstacles breed discord, hindering overall productivity.
- Respect is pivotal in leader-employee dynamics, minimizing hostility and encouraging cooperation.
- Avoiding humiliating tactics prevents counterproductive behaviour.
- Meritocracy values results over agreeability, promoting genuine feedback and diverse perspectives.
- Leaders prioritize earning respect over seeking fleeting popularity, fostering enduring commitment.
- Trust, accountability and shared goal-setting build ownership and commitment toward shared objectives.

In essence, leaders shape organizational culture through their actions and decisions. Principles of mutual benefit, respect, fairness and accountability foster collaboration, driving sustained success.

THE HAZARDS OF SUCCESS

In life's complex tapestry, managing success and failure is a profound challenge. Winners understand this dichotomy and embrace constant learning and adaptation. Yet, pitfalls arise when success is presumed, and a lack of a positive attitude undermines adaptability.

Patterns emerge in the setbacks of some; they miss opportunities due to a failure to learn from mistakes. Vague goals obscure their path, diluting their pursuit and causing uncertainty.

A lack of strong alliances, materialism and resistance to change hinder growth. Inability to rebound from setbacks and underutilization of strengths magnify weaknesses.

The crucial lesson here is never to underestimate attitude. Winners attribute their success to attitude, the linchpin setting them apart. Our response to life's cues shapes our trajectory, underscoring the importance of cultivating a positive, adaptable attitude for lasting success.

Do you wish for greater acceptance?
Think Positively to brighten personality.
Do you wish to be more successful?
Think Positively to develop your career.
Do you wish to have more ability?
Think Positively to improve your skills.
Do you wish to be happier?
Think Positively to improve your judgments.
Do you wish your life to be better tomorrow?
Think Positive thoughts today.

'Attitude is the scale on which we balance our strengths and limitations. Outside circumstances are less important in the long run than our inner view of our selves.'